The
SEARCH
FOR GRACE

D0880574

The
SEARCH
FOR GRACE

A DOCUMENTED CASE
OF MURDER
AND REINCARNATION

by

DR. BRUCE GOLDBERG

IN PRINT PUBLISHING

Published by IN PRINT PUBLISHING
65 Verde Valley School Road #F2
Sedona, Arizona 86351

Cover design and illustration: Howard Goldstein Design
Photo: Ellis J. Malashuk, courtesy of The Baltimore Sun Company,
copyright © 1982 The Baltimore Sun

Preassigned LCCN: 94-076641

ISBN 0-9630485-8-9

Manufactured in the United States of America
by Griffin Printing, Penny Hancock
Sacramento, CA

Also By Dr. Bruce Goldberg:

Past Lives–Future Lives

* * * * * * * *

"I have had the pleasure of reviewing Dr. Bruce Goldberg's new book and I am delighted to be able to recommend it, especially to [those] who are interested in exploring exciting altered states of awareness. However we conceive them—whether levels of the mind ordinarily excluded from consciousness or exotic other dimensions of reality—many more of us these days are defying antiquated prohibitions and seeking to decide for ourselves about these uncanny experiences."

—Raymond A. Moody, Jr., M.D.,
author of *Reunions* and *The Light Beyond*

PROLOGUE

Tuesday night, May 17, 1927. She had ditched her husband Chester (the boring) Doze, and gone shopping. Her new bobbed haircut, short, sexy skirt and red shoes were everything Chester hated–and Jake loved. But she had been waiting in the street for fifteen minutes, and when Jake picked her up he looked like he'd had more than a few drinks.

Jake's bad temper was showing; during the drive their discussion rapidly escalated into a heated argument.

> *Jake.* You know what the guys were talking about at the bar? I had to hear about all the men you've slept with. I hear you're still sleeping around.
>
> *Grace.* That's a lie.
>
> *Jake.* Look at that outfit you're wearing. I think you look like a cheap tart right now.

> Grace. And I think you're drunk, probably too drunk to
> show me a good time tonight. (Mocking laugh-
> ter.)

*Without warning, Jake punched her with his right hand, square
on her jaw. She was conscious but in pain.*

> Grace. What are you stopping for, you bastard?

> Jake. I'm going to teach you not to laugh at me. I'm go-
> ing to teach you real good.

*Jake strangled Grace, beating her badly. The next day her body was
found in Ellicott Creek.*

I guided her to the superconscious mind level.

> Dr. G. Grace, do you know Jake in your current life as
> Ivy?

> Ivy. Yes, he's John.

*John (Jake), who had murdered Ivy (Grace) in 20 of the 46 past
lives uncovered through hypnosis, had begun beating her in her present
life. She wanted desperately to break off the relationship and end the
recurrent nightmares from which she awoke screaming in terror, murdered over and over by the same mysterious man—but she just couldn't
seem to pull herself free. Where would it end? Was there any way she
could escape this karmic whirlpool before she drowned...again?*

* * * * * * * *

Tuesday night, May 17th, 1994. TV viewers across America
clicked idly through the channels looking for prime-time entertainment. Many settled on the TV movie *Search for Grace*, a thriller
about an attractive young woman trapped by an overwhelming
magnetism for a powerful, suspicious stranger who turns physically abusive. Seeking psychological therapy for this irrational

compulsion and related nightmares, Ivy is hypnotically regressed. She begins to recount, in trance, the events leading to the brutal death, more than half a century past, of a woman she has never heard of in a place she has never been. Her confusion and terror mount as she finds that the woman, Grace Lovel, did indeed live—and die—exactly as she has related. And that Grace's murderous boyfriend, Jake, has an uncanny resemblance to her violent new lover, John.

The fictionalized TV production, though billed as "inspired by an actual case history," made no further reference to the stranger-than-fiction true story of the real Ivy. A patient of the renowned hypnotherapist Dr. Bruce Goldberg, her past-life regressions revealed an eternal love-triangle, a terrifying karmic dance of passion and murder, culminating in the short, tragic career of one Grace Doze, a headstrong flapper whose reckless love life ended in murder. Only years later did Dr. Goldberg discover that Ivy's account of the smallest details of Grace's life and death could be explicitly documented through contemporary newspapers and police reports.

There was no way the CBS movie could reflect the powerful obsession that brought Ivy back to Dr. Goldberg's office to be regressed again and again, 45 times, long after both doctor and patient felt that their initial therapeutic goals had been achieved. Something in Ivy would not let her rest until she had relived the 46th life and brought to light the circumstances of what the Buffalo, New York, police still listed as an unsolved homicide. Dr. Goldberg himself was fascinated with the strange recurrent coincidences—"synchronicity" in his phrase—that seemed inevitably to draw Grace's tale to the attention of CBS producers, as if it were fated to be aired.

Could it have been the unquiet spirit of the murdered young woman, working through her reincarnation as Ivy, that demanded, at long last, public resolution of the mystery of her death? There is one more coincidence to which the TV production made no allusion:

When *Search for Grace* broadcast the dramatization of her killing on that Tuesday night in May, it was 67 years, *to the hour*, since Grace Doze died.

CONTENTS

FOREWORD

I have practiced hypnotherapy on a full-time basis since 1974, when serendipitous events and "good karma" convinced me to give up dentistry and devote my complete attention to my hypnotherapy practice, specializing in past-life regression and future-life progression. The techniques depicted herein are those I regularly use in my office, and although minor details and all names in the cases described have been altered to protect the privacy of my patients, everything else in these pages is true. It should be pointed out that a regressed patient speaking from a past life will commonly retain his or her current life perspective, which may be reflected in vocabulary, attitude, etc.

It is my hope in this book to illustrate that past-life regression hypnotherapy, now proven in its ability to assist patients in resolving conflicts, can withstand comprehensive objective investigation into the facts surrounding case histories. A greater purpose is to enable you, the reader, to maximize your own potential by tapping into your higher self. The book is therefore dedicated to its readers. Since thought creates reality, every person who open-mindedly reads this book will, in his or her own way, positively influence our ever-expanding universe of consciousness.

—Dr. Bruce Goldberg

ACKNOWLEDGMENTS

I would like first to thank Ivy, Alex Ayres, CBS Television and my publisher, Tomi Keitlen. S.J.Tower, Librarian of Hutchinson Central Technical High School, Michael G. Andrei, Communications Manager of the Greater Buffalo Chamber of Commerce, Santo (Sandy) Constantino, Chief of Detectives of the Buffalo Sheriff's Department, Bob Hark of the Tonawanda Police Department, the Buffalo Historical Society, and others too numerous to mention provided invaluable cooperation in my research. Permission to reprint materials used herein was graciously granted by *The Buffalo News*.

1: SYNCHRONICITY

It was a warm Friday afternoon in late September, 1991, and I was waiting in a producer's office in CBS Television City in Los Angeles to discuss *The Montel Williams Show*. This interview and the events that followed were part of the strange synchronicity that resulted in the CBS movie-for-television, *Search for Grace*, that would air in May, 1994. Synchronicity is the term used by Carl Jung, the psychiatrist and former student of Freud, to refer to meaningful occurrences without apparent causes—what the lay person would term coincidence. In the view of Parapsychology and Transpersonal Psychology, there are no coincidences; every event has a global karmic meaning, and the case presented in this book is no exception.

Television City is located at 7800 Beverly Blvd., in Los Angeles, near my office in Woodland Hills in the San Fernando Valley. Many television shows are taped here, ranging from syndicated talk shows to situation comedies, and CBS's Executive Offices for the West Coast are located in this complex. I should point out that although *The Montel Williams Show* is taped here, CBS has nothing to do with the show, which is distributed by Viacom. However, as a result of this interview and Montel's subsequent past-life regression, a taping was scheduled for Tuesday, October 1, which became a hot topic throughout CBS. When a taping is done at such a studio, anyone in the complex can view the show since closed-circuit television monitors are available throughout the building. So although the actual show was not aired until October 14, CBS employees knew about it as of October 1.

What I didn't know at the time was that the person who would become executive producer for the movie-for-television was soon to have a meeting with a CBS official to pitch the idea. The project was accepted shortly thereafter, and although many other factors were involved in the decision, one cannot ignore the synchronicity of the timing of the *Montel Williams* taping.

In order to demonstrate the technique to the producers, I had been asked to regress a show researcher I will refer to as Mary, a personable, conventional twenty-five-year-old woman. Mary was first regressed to the age of six and reported a pleasant scene sightseeing with her father in downtown Chicago. The positive emotions she expressed during this session surprised her as well as the producers watching the demonstration.

During the past-life regression, a striking incident occurred when Mary deliberately misled a group of men dressed in dark clothes who were interrogating her concerning the location of a male friend of hers, apparently a fugitive falsely convicted of a crime in the United States during the 1940's. The final technique I used was a "superconscious mind tap." After the regression Mary felt "suspended in air" and ethereal, totally at peace with the universe—something an overworked researcher is not used to experiencing on a Friday afternoon.

When the session was concluded, I went to the production office. The producers had requested my input in designing the show due to my experience as a television consultant and frequent talk-show guest. During the meeting, Montel Williams dropped by and was briefed about Mary's experience. He was skeptical about the entire subject and dared me to regress him. I readily accepted the challenge, although he clearly doubted his susceptibility to hypnotic trance, let alone regression. I have learned that this attitude rarely prevents a patient from experiencing regression or progression.

Back in Montel's private office, with his brother as a witness, I began working with him. His age regression took him back to the age of ten, skateboarding down a hill in Baltimore, Maryland. He appeared surprised at his emotions and the clarity with which he remembered the scene. The past-life regression was even more dramatic. He described himself as a slave in the South during the Civil War, wounded and surrounded by four or five white farmers who were about to kill him. Later, on the air, he stated, "I felt very, very nervous and very, very scared." His death at the hands of the farmers is significant in that he is currently involved with many groups aiding underprivileged black children.

This was a very emotional past-life regression for this articulate black man, who strongly identified with the karmic significance of that past life. But although it was intense and interesting, the session was not taped and was only heard of at CBS by word of mouth. It was the regression and progression of one of my patients during actual taping which generated most of the interest.

We shall call this patient Lori, an attractive, thirty-one-year-old businesswoman who came to me for help with her addiction to caffeine and sugar, and with depression. The following are excerpts from the show that illustrate her experiences.

Dr. G. What is your name?

Lori.   Blue Eagle.

Dr. G. What is your occupation?

> Lori.   I am a seer from my tribe.

Lori described a very spiritual life as a seer in Utah during the sixteenth century. She was a male Native American, tall, slim, and muscular, with long black hair. I moved her forward to an event she would consider significant.

> Dr. G.   Blue Eagle, where are you now?
>
> Lori.   I am flying as an eagle. I fly to get a different perspective.
>
> Dr. G.   What happens then?
>
> Lori.   I am able to communicate with other people.
>
> Dr. G.   How do you communicate with these other people?
>
> Lori.   With mind.

Lori described a superconscious mind experience in which she left the body and took the spiritual form of a blue eagle. From this astral plane, she (he) could communicate telepathically with another tribe.

Montel interjected a question to establish the time frame.

> M.   What year are you in?
>
> Lori.   It's 1586.

A scan of other past lives from the superconscious mind level revealed a life Lori had in Atlantis.

> Dr. G.   Can you tell us a little bit about your life in Atlantis?
>
> Lori.   My name is Nomi. I am a woman in something like a hospital. I soothe people after they have an operation.
>
> Dr. G.   What year comes into your mind?

Lori.   30,560 BC.

Nomi was a fifteen-year-old healer who used laying on of hands to effect post-operative care. Surgery did not involve the removal of organs but their repair, using energy from very quiet generators. The hospital was described as a large white building with rounded arches and thick walls. Tumors were cured by "negating their bad energy."

Lori, as Nomi, lived until she was 150 years old, remaining a healer for the rest of this long incarnation. Her description of her death was of a form of energy transfer, free from pain. When I asked her what she learned from that life, she stated, "We are all connected—all one."

Lori was also progressed into a future life during the thirty-first century.

> Dr. G. What is your name?
>
> Lori. Julie.
>
> Dr. G. What year is it, to the best of your knowledge?
>
> Lori. 3070.
>
> Dr. G. What kind of work do you do?
>
> Lori. I am an astronomer.

Lori was then progressed to the significant event of her future life.

> Dr. G. What do you perceive?
>
> Lori. Well, I've gotten some kind of recognition for my work. My husband does the same work, and he is also recognized.

I next progressed her to the last day of her life.

> Dr. G. Now, Julie, tell me what you perceive.

Lori. I was not expected to die. I'm dying very young.

Dr. G. How old are you?

Lori. Forty-five.

Dr. G. What is it you are dying from?

Lori. I'm in a collision in space.

Dr. G. Is your husband with you?

Lori. No, I'm alone.

Lori, as Julie, described a society that needed its consciousness raised. English was the universal language, and though there were no wars, much tension existed in the business world.

When asked what the death experience was like, she responded, "It was very easy. I just left my body, and it was not painful. First, I saw myself sitting, and then my spirit just left." When asked if anyone from any other of her lives is around now, she stated, "Yes, I am currently attracted to the man who was my husband in the year 3070. We are in a platonic relationship now, and I don't want to tell him for fear he will be shocked."

Lori also mentioned some of the age progressions we had done about a year-and-a-half ago concerning her future in this life. Some of the experiences she had perceived then had already occurred since I last saw her. She stated that among the benefits she received from being regressed were the ability to know herself at a deeper level and a significant improvement in her self-image.

While such dramatic material was fascinating to all who saw the tape, it was not simply the impact of this single incident or even its juxtaposition to Montel's experience that accounted for the role CBS played in making *Search for Grace*.

Many months earlier, in 1991, a former executive at CBS News in New York had contacted me with a similar project in mind. This man, whom I will call Tom, was then working as an independent television producer in Los Angeles, where he had heard me on a local radio station. He suggested I screen my files for a documented case that would illustrate a female patient overcoming great adversities through past-life regression hypnotherapy. But after meeting with him and his associate, I decided against the project.

There is an old saying in metaphysics: "When the student is ready, the teacher will be there." Apparently, the timing was not yet right then, but CBS continued to stand out in my mind as part of the matrix of synchronicity, and surfaced again later to make the movie a reality.

2: IN THE BEGINNING

The role CBS played in the realization of *Search for Grace* is clear. But how did it all begin, and when did CBS enter the equation?

In *Past Lives–Future Lives*, I described my work with a Baltimore talk-show host named Harry Martin, whom I regressed to three past lives and progressed into two future lifetimes. When we discussed his experience with hypnosis on his talk show, *Hello Baltimore*, numerous calls came into the studio at WBAL-TV, a CBS affiliate. This was my first media interview, and once again, CBS was involved. Although it may appear that I am stretching the point, circumstances bear out the case for synchronicity.

Prior to *Hello Baltimore*, I had only begun to scale down my dental practice to devote more time to hypnotherapy. It was as a result of these interviews that this process accelerated and I became motivated to write *Past Lives–Future Lives*. *Past Lives–Future Lives*, in turn, brought Ivy, the subject of the television movie, to my practice.

In February, 1983, after my interviews with Harry Martin, the CBS television affiliate in Washington, D.C., WDVM-TV contacted me to do a news story on my work. The producer wanted me to regress one of their reporters, Mike Buchanan. I agreed and the following is an excerpt from the regression that aired.

> Dr. G. Can you tell me where you find yourself?
>
> Mike. A farm.
>
> Dr. G. Can you perceive what you are wearing?
>
> Mike. Farmer's clothes. I'm about 40.
>
> Dr. G. What are you thinking about at this particular time?
>
> Mike. Fear—a natural disaster.

I moved Mike forward to the most significant event in his past life as a farmer.

> Dr. G. What has happened since I last spoke to you?
>
> Mike. Locusts—devastation.
>
> Dr. G. What have you lost as a result of this?
>
> Mike. A crop—corn.
>
> Dr. G. Tell me how you feel.
>
> Mike. Frustration, anxiety, anger.
>
> Dr. G. What year is this?
>
> Mike. 1918.

I then progressed Mike forward to the last day of his life.

> Dr. G. Where are you?
>
> Mike. Omaha, Nebraska, in a bed.

Dr. G.   What are you suffering from?

Mike.   I just don't feel well. I'm just tired.

Dr. G.   How old would you say you are?

Mike.   Eighty.

The broadcast then turned to Mike's follow-up research. It's always impressive when a patient documents part of his past-life regression, but it is even more dramatic when the patient is a skeptical reporter. Mike is from Chicago, most definitely a big-city man. He has never been to nor has he any desire to spend time on a farm. (In light of his past-life history, it is not difficult to see why.) A check of the records at the Iowa State Library in Des Moines showed that in 1918 locusts caused damage to crops in one-half of the counties in Iowa. An Iowa farmer alive in 1918 stated, "In 1918, they [locusts] just about tripled to what they ever were before."

This news report was viewed by a magazine editor in Washington, D.C. named Alex Ayres who had never heard of me before; it is he who wrote the script for *Search for Grace*. But as you will see, a circuitous path was to unwind before Alex and I met.

The next CBS tie-in, later in 1983, again involved WDVM-TV. Carol Randolf, a black lawyer who became a television talk show host, had a show there called *Morning Break*. Her producer approached me about being a guest on the show, and I suggested that I regress Carol in my office prior to appearing live. Everyone agreed, and Carol, her producer, and a news crew from the station came to my office at the end of October. The following is an excerpt from Carol's past-life regression, aired on November 18, 1983.

Dr. G.   Where are you?

Carol.   It's the South.

Dr. G.   What is happening now?

Carol. The Civil War.

Dr. G. Can you describe yourself?

Carol. All I see is hair. It's red.

Dr. G. About how old are you?

Carol. About sixteen. I seem to be rather frivolous. I guess I'm attractive.

I then progressed Carol forward to a significant event.

Dr. G. What has happened?

Carol. Someone is dead.

Dr. G. Someone close to you?

Carol. It must be. I'm dressed in black.

Dr. G. What is your name?

Carol. Sarah.

Dr. G. Whose funeral was it?

Carol. But he has the wrong uniform on.

Dr. G. The man you were mourning was a Northerner?

Carol. Yes. It's confusing.

Carol Randolph used to be a teacher, and in her past life as Sarah she also was a school teacher. Sarah then described her death, lying in bed, very old, surrounded by some of her former pupils, along with her family. She had had a love affair with a Union soldier during the Civil War.

When the show aired live on November 18, 1983, my birthday as it happened, little did I know that a most unusual birthday present was about to be unwrapped. After running the video tape of her regression as Sarah, Carol informed me on the air that she had done some research, pursuing an intuition that she might have been one of her own ancestors. Carol's father and other close relatives couldn't identify any Sarah in their family. But she discovered from her 105-year-old grandmother that Carol's great-great-grandmother was named Sarah and had red hair. This long-lost relative had never been mentioned to Carol before, and, in fact, her grandmother was the only member of her family to know of Sarah's existence. Thus, another partially documented case unexpectedly unfolded on a CBS affiliate.

Alex, the magazine editor I mentioned earlier, just happened to be watching this show and noted my name in his book of people to call. Then, on December 12, 1984, a story on me appeared in the *Washington Post*'s Style section. In preparation for the article, the reporter, Sandy Rovner, was regressed. The following is an excerpt from her account:

> My two experiences with Bruce Goldberg led me in two quite different directions. In one case, I was self-hypnotized by a tape Goldberg provided. In the second instance, I was hypnotized in his presence.
>
> My first "recollection" was this: "I see her kneeling before a clear pool in a vast cavern. The pool is small and oval, an artificial cistern of some sort. She is using it as a mirror, braiding her long black hair. Her skirt is long, woven from flax, perhaps. It is rough, homespun, the color of wheat. Her long, open jacket is elaborately woven of many colors, including metallic threads. Her name is Mala. I see her with many children, some her own, romping under silvery olive trees. Her husband is away fighting in a war. He is tall, bearded, and rides a horse. I feel her pain at the separation. Is she...was she...me?"
>
> My second experience:

"The jungle is dank and smells from wet earth and decaying vegetation. The 13-year-old novice hunter is named Huhnh. It seems that he has always been alone. He was raised in pell-mell fashion by whatever village mother happened to dole out a little extra food, a little extra love. He learned early to hunt, and he often hunted for himself deep in the giant ferns, the twisting vines. It seems that I am Huhnh. Or, perhaps I am making him up. I cannot be sure."

Under Goldberg's persistent questioning, I follow Huhnh. It is only a few hours after he has discovered himself abandoned by the entire village, and he is curled up in despair under a giant fern. He is dying. He is, I say, in response to Goldberg's questioning, dying from bug bites. I hate bugs. Especially spiders. It is undeniably a powerful experience. I come back to myself with tears on my face.

Alex read this article and called me to inquire about my services; he felt therapy might be valuable for a friend of his. I sent him some information but did not hear from him or his friend, yet.

A further synchronicity had to occur before Alex and I were to meet, and, as you may have guessed, CBS would be involved. One of their producers read the *Washington Post* article and invited me to appear on *Nightwatch*. During the interview, they played part of Carol Randolph's past-life regression as Sarah. When Alex saw this interview on December 27, 1984, he was finally motivated to contact me.

Alex came to my office accompanying his friend, Jean, whom he had referred for therapy. She was treated quickly, and I enjoyed working with her. Alex brought her to each session and eventually asked me if I would be interested in being included in a book he was outlining on reincarnation in the United States. I agreed to participate, and he interviewed me a few times. Although the book never got off the ground, it was becoming clear that Alex was destined to do some kind of project with me. But timing is everything in life, and although the eye of CBS was definitely shining on me, the timing wasn't quite right just yet.

In the early part of 1989, I moved from Baltimore to Los Angeles. I hadn't heard from Alex in a few years, so you can imagine my surprise when I received a letter from him in December, 1989, that had been forwarded from Baltimore to Los Angeles. This time Alex informed me that he had read the second, enlarged edition of my book and wanted to do a television show. I was interested but when I didn't hear from him again, I went ahead with other projects. Then in June, 1991, he called me and restated his interest in doing a movie-for-television. Meetings with the executive producer and others finally resulted in *Search for Grace*.

But it remains to relate how Ivy, the main character of this book and the heroine of the movie, came to be a patient of mine. Naturally, CBS was indirectly involved, through synchronicity.

3: ENTER IVY

Ivy was a 26-year-old pharmacist when I met her. This neat, organized, considerate young woman was very easy to work with, although extremely shy due to repressed feelings later explained by her past lives. I eventually guided her through forty-six regressions, never suspecting how significant one of them was to become. It was, of course, a TV broadcast that first brought us together.

In April 1987 I received a call from one of Oprah Winfrey's producers, who wanted me to fly to Chicago the following week to do her show. I readily agreed, very much looking forward to the experience. The producers asked me if I would conduct past-life regressions on two members of the studio audience. I had about thirty minutes to work with the two women before the show. The following is what transpired:

Dr. G. Can you tell me where you find yourself?

Robin. I am standing at the edge of a jungle.

Dr. G. Can you describe yourself physically?

Robin. I'm a young man. I'm tall and slender and I have dark skin.

Dr. G. What do people call you?

Robin. Saji.

I progressed Saji forward to a significant event, and he described a ritual that greatly upset him.

Dr. G. What is happening now?

Robin. There is a man who is the leader of our people, and he is going to make a sacrifice. The sacrifice (Robin grows very emotional) is my mother.

Dr. G. Have you had problems with this man before?

Robin. No, he's my friend, and I feel betrayed.

I moved Saji forward to the resolution of this event.

Dr. G. What is going on now?

Robin. I'm trying to stop him, but they're holding me back. I'm screaming and trying to stop him.

Dr. G. Does your mother communicate with you at this time?

Robin. She says she's ready to die. It doesn't bother her.

Dr. G. What happens next?

Robin. He is holding a big dagger over his head. I pushed him and he stabs me in the shoulder. I don't even acknowledge it. I feel so outraged. I want to protect her.

Dr. G.   You don't feel the pain then?

Robin.   No. I just keep pushing him. She tells me to let her pass on.

Dr. G.   Is she sacrificed?

Robin.   Yeah, she is sacrificed. I let him do it.

Dr. G.   What about your shoulder?

Robin.   The shoulder bothers me later. It looks like some sort of fungus is there. I feel very bitter about them sacrificing her. I feel guilty because I should have stopped it.

Dr. G.   How did your people treat you after this sacrifice?

Robin.   Because I finally let them do it, it wasn't quite as bad. They would have killed me, too, if I would have stopped it.

Dr. G.   What did you do then?

Robin.   I decided I'm going to walk off and live by myself.

Robin, as Saji, left the village and went to stay with a yoga master. Unfortunately, the shoulder wound became worse and Saji died a few months later. This traumatic life occurred in early India.

From the superconscious mind level I further questioned Saji.

Dr. G.   What did you learn from this life?

Robin.   I learned what it is like to be at peace, but only at the very end of my life.

Saji's mother in that past life turned out to be Robin's best friend in this life, though there were no other karmic ties.

The next studio member to be regressed was Dana. She was a very spiritual woman in her mid-forties, and a pleasure to work with.

> Dr. G. Where are you?
>
> Dana. In a garden.
>
> Dr. G. Can you describe yourself?
>
> Dana. A female in a robe. I have a feeling of happiness.

I then moved Dana forward to a significant event.

> Dr. G. What has happened since I last spoke to you?
>
> Dana. There has been much internal strife over religious differences.
>
> Dr. G. How did this end up?
>
> Dana. We worked the problems out among ourselves.
>
> Dr. G. Do you hold some special position with your people?
>
> Dana. I feel I'm outside the group yet very involved with the group.

In fact, Dana was a priestess in ancient Egypt. I progressed her forward.

> Dr. G. What has transpired since I last spoke with you?
>
> Dana. It seems things are good with our people. We are going forward.
>
> Dr. G. What is your philosophy?
>
> Dana. I believe in energy.

Dr. G.   How do you direct or manifest this energy?

Dana.   Reincarnation.

When Ivy saw this show, she became excited. She knew she had to call me and experience her own past lives. But since she lived out of town, she did not yet make her first appointment. It took one additional bit of urging, which came in the form of *The Phil Donahue Show.*

The producer with whom I had worked on *Morning Break* on the CBS affiliate in Washington, D.C., was now with Donahue. She called me in May of 1987 to schedule me for a July interview. *The Donahue Show* flew two of my patients to New York, one of whom, Jane, had been able to lose 108 pounds through therapy and overcome an infertility problem to become the proud mother of two children. On the air, Phil showed a picture of her before she lost weight, along with a photo of her children.

Through past-life regression hypnotherapy, the other patient, Carla, had overcome agoraphobia, a complex fear of social contact that is devastating to the patient and quite difficult to treat using conventional approaches. Agoraphobia sufferers are commonly afraid to leave their home and panic when waiting in lines; Carla had been unable to leave her bedroom. She described the various therapies she had tried unsuccessfully.

Carla related two medieval past lives. In one, she was a wealthy male landowner whose land was confiscated by the Church. He and his daughter were tortured in a dungeon, and though they survived, his daughter went insane. During Carla's other life she was a male whose father forced him to become a priest. He was sent on one of the Crusades, where he witnessed much brutality. The origins of her agoraphobia lay in this repeated exposure to violence and in claustrophobia from the dungeon.

Donahue had me regress a woman, Thea, from the studio audience on the air. The following is an excerpt from that past-life regression:

> Dr. G.   Tell me where you find yourself now.
>
> Thea.   In a house.
>
> Phil.   Whose house is it?
>
> Thea.   It's my aunt's house.
>
> Dr. G.   And what is your name?
>
> Thea.   Emily.
>
> Dr. G.   And, Emily, do you know about what year this is by the way you keep time?
>
> Thea.   1820.
>
> Dr. G.   Okay. What is going on with your life at this time that you would find significant or important to you?
>
> Thea.   She's very sick.
>
> Dr. G.   Your aunt, you mean?
>
> Thea.   Yes.
>
> Dr. G.   Are you close with your aunt?
>
> Thea.   Yes.

I then moved Emily forward to see what happened to her aunt.

> Dr. G.   Now, Emily, tell me what has happened.
>
> Thea.   She died.
>
> Dr. G.   Your aunt?
>
> Thea.   Yes, she was sick.
>
> Dr. G.   How do you feel about her passing?

Thea.   We miss her.

Dr. G.   When you say we, who else is in that house?

Thea.   My sister and I.

Dr. G.   What happened to your parents?

Thea.   I don't know.

Next I progressed Emily forward to the most significant event in her life. She described a fire in her house.

Thea.   The children are in the house.

Dr. G.   Okay, bring up those emotions. That's all right, you're protected. Okay.

Thea.   The baby.

Dr. G.   The baby?

Thea.   The baby's in the house.

Dr. G.   This is your daughter's child now?

Thea.   She's gone.

Dr. G.   Your grandchild is gone?

Thea.   She died in the fire.

Dr. G.   Okay, all right.

Phil.   Where are we now, time-wise? When, at what period?

Dr. G.   This is the 1830's in the Southeastern United States, and her house was on fire. Her granddaughter was trapped in the house and has died as a result of the fire.

Thea's spontaneous emotions, combined with the fact that she was selected by Donahue's staff and kept in a different part of the studio between the time I worked with her before the show and air time, made her regression a credible one, in Ivy's opinion.

The last regression I did on *The Donahue Show* was with Jane. Here is an excerpt from her session:

Phil.   Jane has been hypnotized by Dr. Goldberg. This is the young woman who successfully lost weight and became pregnant after that. Two issues that were very confounding to her, and she solved them through past-life hypnotherapy.

Dr. G.   Can you describe what you look like now?

Jane.   I'm a man. I dress like an Eskimo. I wear furs. I have black hair, dark eyes. I'm missing a front tooth.

Dr. G.   All right. Is anything going on in your life that you find particularly difficult or uncomfortable?

Jane.   My wife is having a baby. She suffered for three days.

Dr. G.   How did this make you feel emotionally, her suffering?

Jane.   Guilty.

Dr. G.   You blamed yourself for this, then?

Jane.   Yes.

Dr. G.   Guilty. To the best of your knowledge, by the way you keep time, do you know what year this is?

Jane.   I can't assign a number. Early 1800's, I think.

Dr. G.   All right. You can answer questions from others other than my voice. It's okay.

Phil. Can you describe the village?

Jane. It's small. In the summer we're here. We fish. There's eight or ten huts. We leave in the winter.

Dr. G. Is there a problem with food in your village?

Jane. Not in the summer. The winters are always hard.

The male Eskimo's guilt from the near death of his wife during delivery explained the origin of Jane's infertility, and near-starvation when food was scarce during the winter correlated with her eating issues in her current life.

After this show aired in Ivy's city, she finally called my office and made the appointment that would eventually lead her to discover and document a karmic journey winding through a maze of 45 past lives to the 46th—the short, tragic career of Grace Doze.

4: PASSION IN POLAND

It was impossible not to like Ivy when she first entered my office. Shy and self-conscious, she was polite and displayed excellent upbringing. Ivy also had natural talent for music; without any formal training she could sit down at a piano and play well. Ivy had never been hypnotized and had no previous experience with any form of psychotherapy. Her goal in treatment was to improve her interactions with men, and specifically, to end a destructive on-again, off-again relationship with John, who was becoming both physically and psychologically abusive to her.

Although John was untrustworthy, unpredictable and totally unreliable, she was nevertheless drawn to him. Whenever he would do something cruel or selfish, he always managed to talk his way out of it, and Ivy always forgave him and believed him when he swore it would never happen again. The situation was complicated by the fact that they worked together in a large metropolitan pharmacy, and by the involvement of another man named Dave, who had been dating Ivy sporadically for about a year. He was the opposite of John—gentle, kind, loving, inexperienced with women, and compulsively honest.

Ivy's problem was that despite her rational distaste for John's style, she remained inexplicably attracted to him, even though he had started beating her. She was torn between the simple, straightforward, pure love that Dave offered her and the dangerous, almost masochistic, yet exciting romance that she found with John. Ivy liked Dave but there just was not the same spark there as between her and John. Ivy just couldn't get him out of her mind.

An additional symptom involved nightmares, from which she commonly awakened many times throughout the night, screaming in terror, murdered in many different ways by men who looked different but were still the same mysterious person. She didn't know how to interpret that and couldn't remember enough about the dreams to describe exactly what had happened. All she knew was that they were horrible, and she felt panic whenever she had one.

Ivy felt that by breaking off the relationship with John once and for all she might end her nightmares and resulting insomnia. She hoped eventually to become more assertive, confident and successful in relationships, for while she had always been quite attractive, she turned men off with her insecurities and "baggage." I knew that dreams such as Ivy's are often flashbacks to past lives, so I felt there was a good chance regression hypnotherapy could help her.

The first past-life experience we explored revealed the origin of her talent for piano, but it also turned out to presage her other lives in many ways. The regression illustrated ties with both Dave and John in an eternal love triangle, which would spawn many instances of violence and death. Most significantly for the purposes of this book, Ivy's trance description of her past life was rich in historical details I was later able to document.

After orienting Ivy to my techniques and thoroughly conditioning her, we began this exploration.

Dr. G. Where are you at this time?

Ivy. I am taking piano lessons.

Dr. G. Who is your teacher?

Ivy. His name is Maciej and I am fortunate to be his pupil.

Dr. G. Why is that?

Ivy. Maciej is a very successful composer. He has composed many operas and musical comedies.

Dr. G. What is your name?

Ivy. Sophia.

Dr. G. How long have you been taking lessons?

Ivy. About three years.

Dr. G. Are you good at playing the piano?

Ivy. Maciej says I am doing well, but I know I will never be as good as he.

Dr. G. What year is this?

Ivy. 1803.

Sophia lived in Warsaw, Poland, where she was born in 1782, and wanted to be a professional pianist. She lived with her family in a well-to-do section of town as her father was a successful businessman.

Dr. G. What does your family think of your career goals?

Ivy. They are supportive of me.

Dr. G. It sounds like you don't think you are a very good pianist at this time.

Ivy. I know I will improve. There is no pressure on me to improve immediately. I do work quite hard.

Dr. G. I don't mean to offend you, Sophia, but why does such a successful composer spend time working with an average pianist?

Ivy. I'm not offended. Maciej likes me. He says I remind him of a musical comedy he composed. My name was in the title of the work, and it was created before I was born. I have never heard it but it means a lot to him. He is a good and patient teacher.

Dr. G. Sophia, do you have a boy friend?

Ivy. Yes. I see a man named Jakub.

Dr. G. Tell me about Jakub.

Ivy. Well, it's a strange story. Jakub is a traveling musician and composer.

Dr. G. Do you love him?

Ivy. Yes. Since I met him, I just must be with him. He travels a lot and it's very difficult for me.

Jakub was from a working-class family, and wanted to succeed as a composer to compensate for this background.

Dr. G. How did you meet Jakub?

Ivy. I saw him playing one evening at a music house.

Dr. G.   So, Jakub is a successful musician?

Ivy.   No, not really. This music house caters to lower-class people. Playing there is for experience and survival. It does not connote success by any means.

Dr. G.   What kind of music does Jakub compose?

Ivy.   He is trying to incorporate the folk music with classical composition.

Dr. C.   That sounds like a strange combination.

Ivy.   Oh, no, it's all the rage these days.

Dr. G.   Has he been successful in his work?

Ivy.   No. He is very frustrated. He just can't get a break. I know some day he will succeed.

From what Sophia told me about Jakub, it seemed obvious that he was using her. Jakub was poor and struggling, playing unprestigious out-of-town "gigs" for survival. Sophia came from a wealthy family with many influential connections in the performing arts, as was reflected in her father's ability to arrange lessons for her with a well-known composer.

Dr. G.   Tell me more about your relationship with Jakub.

Ivy.   Jakub is an emotional man. He is very intense in everything he does.

Dr. G.   Can you give me an example?

Ivy.   He is part of the Polish resistance against Russia and the other countries trying to carve up our beautiful land.

Dr. G.   That sounds dangerous.

Ivy.   It is, and he moves around so much that sometimes I hardly see him.

I progressed Sophia forward by a few years and she reported the following:

Dr. G.   What has happened since I last spoke to you?

Ivy.   I don't know what to do.

Dr. G.   What is going on, Sophia?

Ivy.   It's Jakub. We fight all the time.

Dr. G.   What about?

Ivy.   He tells me I should stop taking lessons from Maciej. Jakub is not very respectful to my teacher and calls him "the old man."

Dr. G.   Why is that?

Ivy.   Maciej is over seventy but he still is a fine teacher and gentleman.

Dr. G.   Do you think Jakub is jealous of your teacher?

Ivy.   I hate to admit it but I think he is.

Dr. G.   Has anything changed with Jakub's career since we last spoke?

Ivy.   Not really. He is still struggling. But there are other problems.

Dr. G.   Such as what?

Ivy.   I went to a music hall to hear some folk music, and I saw Jakub there.

Dr. G.   Why is that unusual? Doesn't he play in these places?

Ivy.   Yes, he does, but he told me he was going out of town. He wasn't playing there; he was there with another girl.

Dr. G. What did you do?

Ivy.   I approached him and he acted as if he didn't know me. I was so upset I cried all the way home.

Dr. G. Please continue.

Ivy.   It got worse. He came to see me the following day, and we went for a walk. He hit me many times and told me never to do that again. I was never to approach him like that in a public place.

Dr. G. Why?

Ivy.   Because the girl was supposed to be a contact with a composer he was trying to work with.

Dr. G. And you believed him?

Ivy.   No. I knew he lied to me. I just can't break up with him. Is this love or what?

Dr. G. What did your parents say about your bruises?

Ivy.   I told them I was attacked by a man on the way home from the music hall, and they believed me.

This was a disturbing trend. Jakub's political radicalism suggested a dangerous psychological profile. Lying to Sophia had been bad enough, but this violence and Jakub's ongoing professional failures spelled trouble.

I progressed Sophia forward by a year or so.

Dr. G. Sophia, what year is it now?

Ivy. 1807.

Dr. G. What is going on with you and Jakub?

Ivy. Jakub is not doing anything with music these days. All he talks about is politics.

Dr. G. Is he still involved with the Polish resistance?

Ivy. Yes, even more so. He says Poland is ready to rise up against Russia, and he keeps talking about that Napoleon.

Dr. G. What about Napoleon?

Ivy. Jakub is very angry with the French Emperor. He says that we are ready to join France in a war against Russia, but Napoleon won't let us side with him. Jakub says Napoleon made some deal with the Russian Tsar, and this badly hurt our resistance efforts.

Dr. G. How do you feel about this political situation?

Ivy. Oh, I don't care much for politics. That's for men to discuss. My interests lie in the piano.

By this time Sophia was working regularly as a pianist, playing folk music as well as classical pieces. Her work took her to shabby music halls, but she also played in concert halls. Sophia was still blinded by her "love" for Jakub, whose jealousy and instability were worsened by Sophia's progress in her chosen career.

Dr. G. How does Jakub respond to your moderate professional success?

Ivy.   I can't predict him at all. First, he is happy that I no longer study with Maciej. Now he criticizes me for not doing better in my career.

Dr. G.   It sounds like he is jealous.

Ivy.   I don't really want to think that, but I think you are right. I don't know what I am going to do. I need him.

Jakub had beaten Sophia a few more times. Her parents hated him, correctly guessing that he was responsible for the attacks.

Dr. G.   Sophia, why do you stay in this relationship with Jakub?

Ivy.   I can't explain it. Sometimes I realize it's no good for me, but I just can't seem to end it.

Jakub made peace with Sophia, and she invited him over to her home when her parents were out of town. Sophia was taking a bath, not expecting Jakub for about an hour, when she suddenly heard a knock at the front door. From the window upstairs she could see that Jakub was early. Sophia put on a robe and let him in.

Dr. G.   Tell me what happened next.

Ivy.   I let Jakub in, and he seemed upset.

Dr. G.   What was wrong?

Ivy.   His composition was rejected by a local composer, and this always upset him.

Dr. G.   I thought he wasn't active in music any more.

Ivy.   After he saw me perform a few times, he decided to resubmit some of his work.

Dr. G.   Please go on.

Ivy.   Jakub came in and saw a letter from my former teacher and started yelling at me.

Dr. G.   What was in the letter?

Ivy.   Maciej attended a performance I gave and wrote me a very nice letter telling me how proud he was of me.

Dr. G.   And this upset Jakub?

Ivy.   I have never seen him so angry.

Jakub followed Sophia upstairs, and they argued for about a half hour.

Dr. G.   What happened next?

Ivy.   I was standing by the bath tub, and the next thing I knew, Jakub hit me. I almost fainted. He threw me into the tub and pushed my face under the water.

Dr. G.   Go on.

Ivy.   Jakub...please don't...Jakub....

That was the last thing Sophia remembered. Jakub drowned her that night in a fit of rage.

From the superconscious mind level, I eventually discovered that Maciej was Dave, and Jakub was John. Dave here assumed the part of teacher; his role as her lover would become apparent as other past-life experiences were uncovered. John, on the other hand, played the unpredictable and violent role that would prove to be characteristic of him, acting out his insanely jealous insecurity with Ivy as his victim. His inability to be faithful to Ivy in this life was also a precursor of the karmic conflict between him and Ivy. Even the attitudes toward politics expressed here would have later significance. While Jakub was a political activist, Sophia remained detached and disinterested in matters of state. As we shall see, Ivy would become involved in politics, with negative consequences, in other lifetimes.

I later found that historical research quickly uncovered some very interesting evidence authenticating many of Sophia's observations about the culture and music of Poland during her lifetime. In H.G. Wells' *The Outline of History* (784–785), I noted the following background information concerning Poland's political history during the reign of Napoleon:

> There seems to have been as little reason in the foreign policy that now plunged Europe into a fresh cycle of wars. Having quarreled with Great Britain too soon, Napoleon (1804) assembled a vast army at Boulogne for the conquest of England, regardless of the naval situation.... Although Austria and Prussia were broken, Russia was still a fighting power, and the next year was devoted to his tougher and less accessible antagonist.... As yet, he had never touched Russian soil; the Russians were still as unbeaten as the British; but now came an extraordinary piece of good fortune for Napoleon. By a mixture of boasting, subtlety and flattery, he won over the young and ambitious Tsar Alexander I—he was just thirty years old—to an alliance.... Close at hand was Poland, ready to rise up and become the passionate ally of France had Napoleon but willed it so. But he was blind to Poland.

Stefan Jarocinkski's *Polish Music* (382–385) provides extremely specific detail about the cultural and artistic milieu Sophia described.

> [As a] result of the consciously realized ideas of national art, professed by the patriotic and progressive part of the society [and the] natural

> introducing of elements of folk music into the composed "academic music" by plebeian and town musicians to whom folk music was everyday food....elements of folk music and classical style were blended together in such a way that folk melodic patterns were introduced into the thematic scheme of the compositions which, however, were shaped in accordance with the composing schemes and technique of construction cultivated by the classical composers. The rhythms of Polish dance (the polonaise, the mazurka, the krakowiak) and the augmented Lydian fourth which is used in the melodic design testify to the national character of the music. New concert halls open to the general public were built. Numerous virtuosi and famous composers who had visited Poland during Stanislaw August's reign after 1800 frequently displayed their skills before the new middle-class audiences.
>
> Under these favorable conditions a new type of musician appeared; namely, that of the professional musician (whose aim and function was to work for the society). It was, however, a peculiar feature of the Polish musical life of the period that side by side with the professional musicians, amateur musicians, dilettanti, were active, too. Before 1800 they came mostly from the ranks of aristocrats who cultivated music-making and composition as a kind of cultural pastime, sometimes attaining in this field enduring success.

Most striking is the revelation of the probable identity of Maciej in a later passage (88–89):

In 1778, the first original Polish opera was performed in Warsaw on the stage of the National Theater....Its libretto was adapted by Boguslawski from Franciszek Bohomolec's cantata, and the music was composed by Maciej Kamienski (1734-1832), a teacher of music from Warsaw, a Slovak by origin who composed many Polish operas that enjoyed great success. [This] started a series of operas that proved most characteristic of Polish composition of the era of Enlightenment. As in other dramatic works, above all in the comedies so enthusiastically produced at Polish theaters, the plots of the libretti of those operas were based chiefly on rustic themes. They either represented village life and problems, as seen through the prism of the then fashionable idyllic sentimentalism, or from the point of view of the new peasant problem based on social grounds (as example,... *Sophia of the Village Wooing*—1779, with music by M. Kamienski and libretto by S. Szymanski), and it gave the composer new possibilities of introducing elements of folklore into his music.

This is highly suggestive evidence that Ivy's past life as Sophia actually occurred. Ivy is not Polish nor is she knowledgeable about the music of Poland. She has never, in this life, anyway, been to Poland. This was an encouraging start in documenting one of the past lives which were to culminate in the tragic story of Grace Doze.

5: A SHEPHERD OF SOULS

Ivy was very pleased with the results of her first session. She was fascinated by the concept of reincarnation and immediately began to feel a lot better about herself. Even though the first regression had ended in her murder, she felt a cloud beginning to lift. Interestingly, she experienced fewer nightmares than usual during the intervening week. When I next saw her she was ready to continue with past-life regressions, so we began another encounter.

Dr. G. Can you tell me where you find yourself?

Ivy. I...I seem to be a man.

Dr. G. You sound surprised.

Ivy. Well, it's just that I'm not used to thinking of myself from a man's viewpoint. It's a little strange, to say the least.

Dr. G. What kind of environment do you find around you?

Ivy.   I seem to be in a rural environment. There are pastures in the background and many sheep.

Dr. G. How are you dressed?

Ivy.   I am wearing simple clothes, a robe of sorts. Also, I am carrying some sort of pole.

Dr. G. What is your occupation?

Ivy.   A shepherd. I am actually a shepherd. (Patient is very surprised.)

Dr. G. How do you like being a shepherd?

Ivy.   You know, it's funny. You would think this should be a piece of cake.

Dr. G. And it isn't?

Ivy.   That's just it. I feel very pressured. I didn't want to be a shepherd. It's just too much responsibility. There really are a lot of sheep here, and they wander around everywhere.

Dr. G. Why are you a shepherd, then, if you don't like it?

Ivy.   My family are all shepherds. I don't really have a choice. I must tend to these sheep whether I like it or not.

Dr. G. To the best of your knowledge, what year is it?

Ivy.   1308.

Dr. G. Do you know where you are?

Ivy.   It seems to be Southern France.

Dr. G.   What is your name?

Ivy.   Claude.

Dr. G.   Claude, have you told your father that you just don't like being a shepherd?

Ivy.   No. I am very timid. The other men in our group make fun of me. They say I'm weak and a coward.

Dr. G.   Are you?

Ivy.   I don't know.

Claude seemed to be afflicted with Ivy's characteristic lack of assertiveness. He meant well but just couldn't get his act together. Being the laughing stock of his people didn't help his already low self-image.

I next progressed him forward to a significant event.

Dr. G.   What has transpired since I last spoke with you?

Ivy.   I really don't like my life. All I do is watch over these stupid sheep. It's so boring. I can't even do that right. Many times my negligence results in sheep wandering.

Dr. G.   What does your family do about this?

Ivy.   Oh, they try to help me, but I think even they have given up on me amounting to anything.

Dr. G.   Is there anyone, outside of your family, that is important to you?

Ivy.   Yes. There is a girl that I like. She is a few
years younger. (Claude is eighteen). But I
am afraid of her.

Dr. G.   What do you mean, afraid of her?

Ivy.   Well, she's a girl, and I just can't bring myself
to talk to her.

Dr. G.   Does she know you?

Ivy.   Well, she knows that I tend sheep here, but
she has never spoken to me.

Dr. G.   What about your family?

Ivy.   They all know that I like her. In fact, my brothers and sisters laugh about it behind my
back. Sometimes I can hear them, and I
run off and cry.

Claude was miserable. No matter what he did, he failed. He
couldn't tend sheep. He wasn't able to communicate his feelings
to a girl he cared for. Claude positioned himself as a hopeless
incompetent who quickly became the laughing stock of his
community. It is no wonder that he was depressed most of the
time.

Dr. G.   Claude, you say you don't like being a shepherd. What would you rather be doing instead?

Ivy.   I like music. I'd rather make music.

Claude described a sort of lute or primitive guitar that he
played. He loved playing this instrument; the problem was that
he played it too much. Sometimes he would become so involved
with playing that he would ignore his duties. That is when he
would lose sheep, which resulted in conflicts with his father. It is
interesting to note that although this life occurred five hundred

years before that of the Polish pianist, already karmic patterns were emerging in relationship to musical interest and talent.

As I progressed Claude through the next few years, little had altered. I asked him to move to an event that would represent a significant change in his life.

> Dr. G. Where are you now?

> Ivy. I'm still tending sheep but it is getting late, and I am scared.

> Dr. G. What exactly are you afraid of?

> Ivy. I was lost in my music. I mean, I really enjoy playing and my mind just wanders away. You know how it is.

> Dr. G. You said you were scared. Scared of what?

> Ivy. It is one of my many responsibilities to monitor the sheep so they keep away from a certain drinking hole.

> Dr. G. What do you mean?

> Ivy. Well, it's summer and naturally the sheep drink more water. There is one particular spring that is poisonous. I mean, any sheep that drinks from it might shortly die. We can't eat them or we will get sick and die, too, so it is a disaster to let them near this hole.

> Dr. G. So why is that a problem? Don't you keep them far enough away so that they don't drink from this hole?

> Ivy. Yes, of course. But this particular afternoon I got too involved with my music, and a whole bunch of the flock wandered off

> without me knowing about it. I mean, a lot
> of them wandered off.

Dr. G.   Where did they go?

Ivy.   They went to that drinking hole and many of
them got sick. I don't know what to do.
My father has warned me about this too
many times. I'm scared that he will send
me away. I'm afraid to face him.

Claude did finally go back to his family missing many of the
sheep he had started out with. His father was furious. When
Claude tried to explain, his father took his lute and broke it in
half, then threw the pieces at him.

Claude was banished from his family in utter disgrace. He
left, not knowing where to go. In his wanderings, he kept thinking
of all the mistakes he made in his life. He was a lousy shepherd.
He was irresponsible, cowardly, and unable to communicate
with, or earn the respect of others. The only thing he could do
well was play the lute, and even that was now destroyed. He
actually contemplated suicide, but lacked the courage to end his
life. Claude decided to get as far away from his people as he could
and start over. He had absolutely no idea what he was going to
do, but he knew what he was not going to do: Claude would never
again be a shepherd.

After quite a bit of traveling, he wandered into a small
village. He looked around this new place and felt at home.
Nobody knew him here. He could start over. One thing that
caught his attention was the local church. Claude didn't know
what it was, but he somehow felt drawn towards it.

Dr. G.   Claude, what have you been up to?

Ivy.   I feel better about myself now.

Dr. G.   What are you doing with your time?

Ivy.   I work at the local inn. I clean up after the customers.

Dr. G   Do you enjoy this?

Ivy.   Yes, I would say that I do like this. It's a lot better than chasing sheep around the countryside.

Dr. G.   Have you made any friends?

Ivy.   Yes, other than the owner of the inn, I talk to the Friar.

Dr. G.   Do you mean as in confession?

Ivy.   No, I mean as a friend. The Friar comes into the inn sometimes and we talk. He knows I'm new in town, so I guess he feels he should help me adjust to this place.

Dr. G.   What do you talk about?

Ivy.   Oh, just about anything. He really is easy to talk to. People tend to only see him when they have a problem or on Sunday.

Dr. G.   So you are both in the same boat? What I mean is that you both desire someone to talk to, and you have something in common?

Ivy.   You mean because we both are losers?

Dr. G.   No. Go on.

Ivy.   Well, he asks me about my belief in God, and I don't know what to tell him.

Dr. G.   Why is this so difficult?

Ivy.   I guess it's because I never really gave it much thought. I mean, I do believe in God. I am a God-fearing Christian, but I don't like to think of death and an afterlife.

Dr. G.   Why do you think he asks you these questions?

Ivy.   He seems to think that I am smart. Imagine that. This educated man of the Church thinks I am smart. He is encouraging me to enter the Church. You know, become a friar.

Dr. G.   Is that what you want to do?

Ivy.   I don't know. But I do enjoy our conversations.

As time went on, Claude became comfortable with his new life. He had no contact with anyone from his past. He liked his job at the inn and enjoyed the talks he had with the Friar. Claude gained confidence in himself and began to communicate well with people of the town. He could even talk to the women. He wasn't romantically involved with anyone, but they all seemed to like him, and he liked them. Once in a while, Claude would ponder about what the priesthood would be like.

Eventually Claude decided to enter holy orders. It was a difficult decision, but once he made it, he began a new life. He studied at a monastery for years. Although the regimen was difficult, Claude worked hard. He showed that he was responsible and committed to the task. The rigorous discipline required didn't seem to dissuade Claude. He learned his lessons and showed compassion to all whom he counseled.

To hear Claude after he was ordained was to witness a metamorphosis. He now was ready to help others and eagerly accepted his vocation. Although he requested to be assigned to the small town he had stayed in while working at the inn, that was not to be. His parish was about one hundred miles away, and Claude never again returned to that village. Life in his new location was hard. He was assigned to work at a church with an older colleague. This friar was not easy to get along with, seeming to resent Claude's youthful vigor and competence. Perhaps the older friar expected Claude to be unsure of himself and seek the guidance of his superior, as he once would have, but now Claude was a very different man. He had matured physically, emotionally, and spiritually. The skinny, almost emaciated teenager had put on weight and apparently had a nice physique. He even described himself as a handsome man and said others had also described him so.

Claude's self-confidence was high. He knew what to do and how to do it. It was not that he ignored his colleague; he just didn't need to consult with him as much as the rather demanding cleric wished.

Dr. G. Do you have any run-ins with this man?

Ivy. Not in that sense. It's indirect.

Dr. G. How so?

Ivy. We never have verbal arguments as such. He seems to feel threatened by my presence and takes every opportunity to undermine me.

Dr. G. In what way?

Ivy. He criticizes me behind my back. Sometimes he tells people to ignore what I said and do the opposite.

Dr. G. Have you done anything to him to bring this about?

Ivy. Honestly, no. I can't think of anything I could possibly have done that would merit this response. It's almost as if he was out to get me from the very start.

I did not interpret this statement as paranoia. Claude's credibility was excellent, and what he reported followed a recognizable pattern. The older friar was apparently unsure of himself and didn't seem to like people much. Perhaps he saw Claude as a manifestation of his own lost youth; more likely, he was jealous of Claude's natural competence as a counselor and his popularity with the townspeople. This fits logically with the insecurity clearly exhibited by the old gentleman.

> Dr. G. Can you talk to the other friar about this situation?
>
> Ivy. Of course I have tried. I have done everything I can think of to resolve this.
>
> Dr. G. What does he say to you?
>
> Ivy. He ignores me. Either he will change the topic or he tells me that I can't possibly understand these duties at my young age.
>
> Dr. G. It sounds like you can't win. Doesn't this depress you day after day?
>
> Ivy. No, I can't say that it depresses me. However, it is a rather frustrating situation. I can handle it, but I am worried about the people.
>
> Dr. G. What, specifically, are you concerned about?
>
> Ivy. He tells the people to ignore what I say. They respect me too much to just accept that, but it is confusing for them. They don't know who to listen to about very important personal problems. This is not good.

As time went by, things settled down. Claude had fewer problems with the friar. It seems that Claude's popularity with the townspeople had a lot to do with this peace. His superior didn't want to cause trouble as their order was very strict, and he wished to keep up appearances for the visits to the parish made by Church officials. The last thing the older priest wanted was to have to explain disharmony to a bishop.

> Dr. G.   Are you able to talk about the older friar's background?
>
> Ivy.   Yes, once in a while he opens up to me.
>
> Dr. G.   What kind of things does he tell you?
>
> Ivy.   He came from a well-to-do family. He fell in love with a young girl from his village and planned to marry her.
>
> Dr. G.   What happened?
>
> Ivy.   Apparently his father felt he was too immature for marriage and did not approve of the young man's choice in a mate.
>
> Dr. G.   So, what did the priest's father do to put a stop to this?
>
> Ivy.   He forced him to go to a monastery and become a friar.
>
> Dr. G.   You mean he didn't want to be a friar at all?
>
> Ivy.   No. He also told me that his father favored his older brother, and this upset him even more.

Now we had a much more thorough insight into the older friar. He resented Claude's enthusiasm for the Church, which he had been forced to join. He also resented the fact that Claude was well thought of and respected by the townspeople. Remember, the older friar's father showed him little respect, and even the townspeople barely tolerated his negative attitudes. Kindness and compassion are necessary to be an effective clergyman, and the elder cleric's crusty personality just didn't fill the bill. To his irritation, he found he needed Claude to more effectively manage the parish.

I next moved Claude to an event that would be significant in relationship to his career.

Dr. G.   What has happened since I last spoke to you?

Ivy.   I started counseling one of the younger women from the village. She had a lot of problems and could never talk to the other friar.

Dr. G.   What happened?

Ivy.   She felt very comfortable with me and told me a lot about herself.

Dr. G.   Were you able to help her?

Ivy.   Yes, but it's much more complicated than that.

Dr. G.   Tell me about it.

Ivy.   Well, the other friar had dealt with her before, and she preferred to talk with me.

Dr. G.   So you feel he felt slighted?

Ivy.   Yes. He was quite upset about the situation.

Dr. G.   Did he talk to you about it?

Ivy.   Yes, he did. The problem is how we discussed her.

As it developed, the old friar had become very jealous of anything Claude did. The girl, Marie, daughter of a local farmer, spent a lot of time in town and always spoke highly of Claude. The older friar resented this and made further misinterpretations that bothered Claude. Marie was a very attractive seventeen-year-old girl, and Claude was a handsome man. The friar concluded they were romantically attracted. This would cause many problems for Claude if it were believed.

Dr. G.   Did the other priest confront you with these accusations?

Ivy.   At first, no. Later on he became more aggressive in his accusations.

Dr. G.   Did he threaten you?

Ivy.   Not directly, no. He did say that if I kept seeing her, he would do his best to stop me from "using" Marie.

Dr. G.   I have to ask you this question, Claude. It's a very delicate matter, but I must know your motives.

Ivy.   Go ahead. I'll answer any questions.

Dr. G.   Were you attracted sexually to Marie?

Ivy.   I liked Marie. I enjoyed talking to her. But to say that I wanted to be with her physically is wrong.

Dr. G.   Could you be more specific?

Ivy.   Well, I never thought of Marie in that way. Celibacy is an important requirement for my work. I take my professional responsibilities quite seriously. So, to answer your question, I didn't want to be with Marie in any sexual way. No.

Dr. G.   Do you think that Marie was in love with you?

Ivy.   I can't read her mind. All I can say is that she had a lot of problems and felt much better after we talked. She never made any suggestion about physical attraction to me. In fact, the great majority of the things she discussed dealt directly with the stress she felt in life.

Dr. G.   What were some of these other problems you said Marie discussed?

Ivy.   Marie complained of headaches and a "pounding stomach."

Dr. G.   Did others know about these issues?

Ivy.   Oh, yes. The family and most of the town knew about her problems. She was not shy in discussing them.

Dr. G.   Did the other friar know about them?

Ivy.   Yes, he did. That was one of the things that we argued about. He felt that since he couldn't help her, there was little possibility that someone as young as me could be of any assistance.

Dr. G.   So he felt threatened about the rapport you established with Marie?

Ivy.   Yes. Most definitely.

My guess is that the older friar felt a deeper form of resentment. Working and failing with Marie probably reminded him of his youth and of the fiancee he had to give up. Claude's physical attractiveness and the progress he was making with Marie merely added to his insecurity. The friar seemed to be a petty man, capable of doing almost anything to protect his fragile ego.

Another disturbing sign was the intensifying anger the old friar was directing towards Claude. The discussions they had quickly developed into arguments that ended with the other friar yelling and pounding his fist. Claude, in contrast, kept his demeanor very much under control during these episodes. He was a true professional, and even through he was being accused of very serious misconduct, he handled the situation like a gentleman.

I next progressed Claude to the resolution of this issue with Marie and the older friar.

Dr. G. What is happening now?

Ivy.   Things are getting out of control.

Dr. G. What do you mean?

Ivy.   Marie is doing fine. Her headaches have disappeared, and she no longer reports a "pounding stomach."

Dr. G. That sounds like great news. What's the problem?

Ivy.   It's the other friar.

Dr. G. What about him?

Ivy.   He doesn't understand how I could possibly help Marie when he couldn't.

Dr. G. Please go on.

Ivy.   Now, he is accusing me of witchcraft.

Dr. G. Witchcraft?

Ivy.   Yes. It's unbelievable, yet quite serious. Have you any idea what they do to people accused of dealing with magic?

Dr. G. Go on.

Ivy.   They burn them at the stake, especially a member of the Church. This is serious.

Dr. G. What will you do?

Ivy.   I don't know. I just don't know.

Dr. G. Can you reason with the older friar?

Ivy.   No. I tried but he is very stubborn. He seems
        intent on destroying me any way he can.

Dr. G. Is it that bad now?

Ivy.   Yes, I think so. He is beginning to spread ru-
        mors about Marie and me among the
        townspeople. He is saying that we have
        been together physically. He also is start-
        ing to make up stories about me perform-
        ing rituals not accepted by the Church.

Dr. G. Don't the townspeople realize what he is try-
        ing to do?

Ivy.   Yes, I do think they sense his jealousy towards
        me. Fortunately, the people think so
        highly of me that nothing is being done
        about it, but I am worried.

Dr. G. What about Marie's family?

Ivy.   They are very supportive and grateful for her
        improvements. The problem is they don't
        know how her cure happened. They ask
        me to explain it, and I can't.

Marie's symptoms were psychosomatic, caused by the
stresses of day-to-day life, but medicine, as we know it, didn't exist
until the nineteenth century; psychosomatic illness was unheard
of in the fourteenth century. When Marie met Claude, the fact
that she was finally able to talk with someone to whom she could
relate was most therapeutic. But in medieval times, a cure like
this appeared suspicious, and it would not be difficult for an
authority figure such as the older friar, who had lived in this town
for many years, to stir up the townspeople.

I progressed Claude to the final resolution of this problem.

Dr. G. What is going on now, Claude?

Ivy.   He has organized the townspeople against me.

Dr. G. What do you mean?

Ivy.   He has been successful in convincing people
         that I was responsible for last year's bad
         crop and other problems.

Dr. G. Go on.

Ivy.   Well, the townspeople are starting to believe
         him, and Marie is now shunned. I notice
         they are starting to treat me different.

Dr. G. Isn't the other friar supposed to report you
         to the Church and have them investigate
         this matter?

Ivy.   Yes, that's the way it's supposed to be, but we
         are a small parish, and he has tremendous
         power.

Dr. G. What finally does happen?

Ivy.   It's hard to describe.

What happened was that the older friar encouraged a
vigilante group to arrest both Maria and Claude. They held a
mock trial and found them guilty of witchcraft. Their sentence
was to be burned at the stake.

Dr. G. Where are you now?

Ivy.   I'm tied to a pole.

Dr. G. Where's Marie.

Ivy.   She is also tied to a pole near me.

Dr. G. What is happening?

> Ivy.   The flames are everywhere. The pain, the
> pain....

This was one of Ivy's more emotional and vocal death scenes. Claude and Marie died a horrible death in intense heat and suffocating fumes that day—not an attractive way to cross over into spirit.

From the superconscious mind level, I was able to ascertain that the priest who originally befriended Claude was Ivy's current father. The older friar who had Claude killed was John, and Marie was a previous life of Dave.

Subsequent research in *The Outline of History* revealed the following:

> The thirteenth century saw the development of a new institution in the Church, the Papal Inquisition.... with fire and torment the Church set itself, through this instrument, to assail and weaken the human conscience.... Before the thirteenth century, the penalty of death had been inflicted but rarely upon heretics and unbelievers. Now, in a hundred marketplaces in Europe the dignitaries of the Church watched the blackened bodies of its antagonists, for the most part poor and insignificant people, burn and sink pitifully, and their own great mission to mankind burn and sink with them into dust and ashes.

Thus, even if they cannot fully validate it, historical records lend credibility to this past life. Numerous outstanding examples of explicit documentation will indeed be cited when I present Ivy's live as Grace Doze. But even this second consecutive partial validation of a past life is impressive. Most regressions are far less endowed with details that can support documentation. A validation pattern was emerging in Ivy's past lives, along with the karmic victim-perpetrator triangle between Ivy, John, and Dave. Of that there was to be much more later.

6: A REVOLUTIONARY SPY

At our next meeting Ivy's progress seemed to be impressive. Though I had seen her only a few times, she was already behaving in a manner that was therapeutically significant. Ivy had a close relationship with her parents and, despite some conflicts, with her sister; all supported her actions and tried not to interfere with her personal life. It was clear that John was not a nice man, but they let Ivy make up her own mind. So it was Ivy herself who had decided her affair with John had to end and was now making a practical assesment of what she knew was going to be a difficult transition. Prior to this time, she had never even considered how to end this admittedly destructive relationship. This was an excellent start, and her self-image had already improved.

Formerly, John had always easily manipulated Ivy. He knew her vulnerabilities and inevitably seemed to get what he wanted from her—not mere sexual gratification; he wanted her soul. John always managed to say the right thing at the right time, and no matter how cruel his actions were, Ivy had typically forgiven him.

However, things were beginning to change. Ivy resisted John's "sweet talking" and refused to see him on demand. The days when Ivy would let John do whatever he wanted, whenever he wanted, were over. Though the case was a long way from being resolved, I was encouraged by this breakthrough.

Ivy didn't have as many questions prior to this hypnosis as in past sessions. She was beginning to understand what was going on and enjoyed the process.

Dr. G.   Where do you find yourself?

Ivy.   I am in a printing shop of sorts. It is not a large building. I see myself working there.

Dr. G.   What is your job there?

Ivy.   I am an apprentice printer.

Dr. G.   Do you enjoy this?

Ivy.   Yes, I do. It's kind of fun putting words in print so people can read about current events.

Dr. G.   What is your name?

Ivy.   Thomas.

Dr. G.   Do you know what year it is?

Ivy.   1777.

Dr. G.   Where to you live?

Ivy.   Williamsburg. Williamsburg, Virginia.

Dr. G.   Do you like your boss?

Ivy.   Yes. We get along fine. He talks a lot about the war, and we run editorial opinions in support of it.

This was, of course, the American Revolutionary War that began in 1775 and ended in 1783. During this time, many colonists were pro-British. Only about one-third of the population openly sympathized with the rebels. Thomas's boss was one of them, an activist who expressed his anti-British opinions in print regularly, although many other newspapers held similar editorial positions.

Dr. G.   What are your feelings about the war?

Ivy.   I don't really get involved with politics. I would like us to be independent of England, but I am not as outspoken about it as my boss.

Dr. G.   Tell me about yourself. Do you have a large family?

Ivy.   No. I am an only child. My parents are farmers.

Dr. G.   How old are you?

Ivy.   I'm twenty.

Dr. G.   Do you have a girlfriend?

Ivy.   Yes, I do. Her name is Abigale, and she is the most beautiful woman in the world.

Dr. G.   Does Abigale talk much about politics?

Ivy.   Heavens, no. She is just interested in girl things.

Dr. G.   Is she supportive of you?

Ivy.   Oh, yes. Abigale encourages me to improve all the time. We never argue about anything. Even if I disagree with what my boss printed in the paper, she backs me up.

Thomas and Abigale made a cute couple. They complemented each other's personalities; whereas Thomas was somewhat shy and quiet, Abigale was more outspoken and social. She urged Thomas to better himself and was his frequent companion. The relationship was almost ideal. Rarely did they have disagreements, and when they did, they were settled quickly and to their mutual satisfaction. Thomas truly loved Abigale, and Abigale deeply cared for him.

> Dr. G. Do you plan to marry Abigale?
>
> Ivy. Yes, as soon as I get my promotion.

Williamsburg was a growing town in the latter part of the eighteenth century. Productive farmland surrounded the city, and many new people arrived in town.

I moved Thomas ahead to a significant event in this past life.

> Dr. G. What has transpired since I last spoke to you?
>
> Ivy. Abigale and I are married. I got my promotion, and we got hitched.
>
> Dr. G. Are you happy?
>
> Ivy. Yes, very happy. So is she. We love each other so much that I almost forget what is going on around us.
>
> Dr. G. You mean the war?
>
> Ivy. Yes, of course. That is all people talk about. When we hear news of a battle, it is argued about at the tavern, and people take sides. You know, some people want England to win; others want us to be free.
>
> Dr. G. Does this lead to problems?
>
> Ivy. Sure, it does. There are all kinds of fights, and sometimes people get killed just for expressing an opinion.

Dr. G.   Do you get involved with these discussions?

Ivy.   No, I just hear about them. I'd rather spend time with Abigale.

Dr. G.   Have you discussed having children with your wife?

Ivy.   Yeah. We decided to wait awhile. We would rather wait until the war is over. This is a tough time to raise kids.

It was indeed a difficult time to live. The townspeople were very divided politically, and even those who tried to remain neutral were dragged into the fray. Fights would begin over contests for the sympathies of citizens unwilling to take sides, since they always involved someone's heated opinion. Then there was Thomas's boss, who was not shy about his opinions. He wrote very pro-colonist editorials and staunchly defended them at the local tavern. It was not unusual for him to get into fights over politics, and he pressured Thomas to side with him during the discussions they had at the print shop.

All in all, though, things were going along relatively smoothly in Thomas's life. I next progressed him forward to an event representing a change.

Dr. G.   Where are you now?

Ivy.   I'm at work.

Dr. G.   Is there anything special about today?

Ivy.   Yes, there is. A lady named Katherine came into the shop to place some notices.

Dr. G.   What is unusual about that?

Ivy.   Nothing. It's her that I can't figure.

Dr. G.   What about her?

Ivy.   I just have this strange feeling about her. I
know I have never met her before. I just
feel as if I know her.

Dr. G. Are you attracted to her?

Ivy.   In a way I am. She is a very pretty lady, and
she wears fine clothes. She even smells
nice.

Dr. G. How did she respond to you?

Ivy.   That's strange, too. She did her business but
kept giving me these looks. I don't know
how to describe them. It's as if she knows
me from somewhere, but she doesn't say
anything.

Dr. G. Did she talk to you?

Ivy.   After she gave me the information for her
printing, she asked me what I thought
about the war.

Dr. G   What is unusual about that?

Ivy.   A lady just doesn't talk politics with a man.

Dr. G. What did you tell her?

Ivy.   Oh, just the usual. I told her that I wasn't particularly interested in politics. She did ask
me a lot of questions.

Dr. G. Did she tell you her opinions of the war?

Ivy.   You know, it's funny. She asked me all those
questions, but she never told me what her
views were. I have no idea what she thinks
about the war, no idea at all.

Katherine appeared to be feeling Thomas out about his
views. This could be just the politeness of someone new in town,

but the instant attraction did strike me as probably karmic. Knowing Ivy's case history, I suspected that it meant trouble.

I next progressed Thomas forward to another significant event.

> **Dr. G.** Thomas, what is going on at this time?
>
> **Ivy.** It's that lady, Katherine.
>
> **Dr. G.** What about her?
>
> **Ivy.** She has been doing a lot of business in town and uses the paper a lot.
>
> **Dr. G.** Go on.
>
> **Ivy.** Well, she seems to take a special interest in me and my life.
>
> **Dr. G.** You mean romantically?
>
> **Ivy.** No, it's not that simple. You see, every time she comes into the shop, she talks to me about the war and the British.
>
> **Dr. G.** You mean how bad they are?
>
> **Ivy.** No, the opposite. She doesn't just come out and say that she is for England, but she does defend their actions and is very convincing.
>
> **Dr. G.** What kind of effect does this have upon you?
>
> **Ivy.** I like her and I can see her point of view. As I told you, I don't think much about the war, and I don't even pay much attention to the editorials written by my boss.
>
> **Dr. G.** What exactly does she tell you?

Ivy.   She has been living in the colonies for about three years. Her family, at least most of them, are still in England. They are being financially hurt by this war, and the hardship has spread throughout the whole country.

Dr. G.   How does this make you feel?

Ivy.   Well, I don't like that. Before the war began, I never disliked the crown. I mean, they never bothered me, and like Katherine says, they founded this country. England built the towns and roads and helped make us what we are today.

Dr. G.   Do you express these sentiments to Katherine?

Ivy.   Yes, I agree with her on many issues.

By this time, a pattern was surfacing. Katherine was definitely a British sympathizer; her family had vested interests in putting down the American revolt. Later, Katherine told Thomas that some of her relations in England were involved in the military. He didn't think that was important, but I saw it as very significant and dangerous. Katherine seemed to be systematically manipulating Thomas to accept her views, and Thomas was just too naive to see this. His attraction for her grew daily. Although he would not readily admit it, he was becoming infatuated with her.

Dr. G.   Does your friendship with Katherine cause any problems with your wife, Abigale?

Ivy.   No, not at this time. Abigale doesn't seem to notice. I never talk to her about Katherine.

Dr. G.   What about your boss? Doesn't he ever talk to Abigale?

Ivy.   Abigale doesn't come into the shop often.
       When she has come in, Katherine wasn't
       here. My boss is only interested in the ex-
       tra business Katherine gives him. Since
       Katherine shows so much interest in me,
       my boss just figures it's good business.

Dr. G. Does Katherine ever discuss politics with
       your boss?

Ivy.   No, she never does.

I wasn't surprised to hear that. Thomas's boss was very
emotional, almost irrational, about his patriotism. Katherine
would be thrown out of the shop if she spoke against the
colonists. If Katherine lied and expressed views in agreement
with the owner of the newspaper, then she ran the risk of losing
her hold on Thomas. Katherine was obviously experienced at
playing a tricky game, and that only boded ill for Thomas.

I progressed Thomas forward to another significant event
in this past life.

Dr. G. What is happening now?

Ivy.   Katherine invited me to a meeting of some of
       her business people.

Dr. G. Is this unusual?

Ivy.   A little. I have only met some of these people
       and only on rare occasions.

Dr. G. Is there anything else unusual about this par-
       ticular meeting?

Ivy.   Yeah, it's going to be held in the evening near
       the edge of town. I never met with these
       people at night before.

Dr. G. Does this concern you?

Ivy.   No, but it is different.

I next progressed Thomas to the meeting and the results of his participation.

Dr. G. What is going on?

Ivy.   This meeting is not what I expected.

Dr. G. In what way?

Ivy.   Well, they are not discussing anything to do with business.

Dr. G. What are they talking about?

Ivy.   The war. They are talking about how I can be of help to them.

Dr. G. And how can you help them?

Ivy.   They want me to be a messenger. I'm supposed to bring messages to certain people and deliver documents to certain offices.

Dr. G. Are you going to do it?

Ivy.   I don't know. I told them I will have to think about it.

I then progressed Thomas forward to his decision.

Dr. G. So, what did you decide to do?

Ivy.   Katherine came to see me often to discuss this. She invited me over to her place, and well, you know.

Dr. G. You mean you made love to her?

Ivy.   Yes. It was beautiful. She really knows how to please a man.

Dr. G. So, what will you do?

Ivy.   Well, since I'm known as a loyal colonist, I won't be as conspicuous as Katherine's people when I travel.

Dr. G.   Where will you travel?

Ivy.   They have a list of places to go. Richmond is the farthest so far.

Dr. G   What about your job?

Ivy.   I know I can't just leave, so I told them I would only make local trips at this time.

Dr. G.   What about Abigale?

Ivy.   I do feel bad about going out on her. I just can't resist Katherine.

Katherine did her best to keep Thomas happy on a string while introducing him to other contacts. She was a British spy and thought nothing of using Thomas to attain her goals. It didn't matter to her that he was risking his family, job, and even his life.

I progressed Thomas forward to the next significant event in this life.

Dr. G.   Where are you now, Thomas?

Ivy.   I am in the print shop.

Dr. G.   What is happening?

Ivy.   My boss is very mad at me.

Dr. G.   Is it your work?

Ivy.   No, it's my other activities.

Dr. G.   You mean he found out about your working for the British?

Ivy.   Yeah, and he is not happy. I have seen him in tavern fights over politics, but I have never seen him this mad at me before.

Dr. G.   Please go on.

Ivy.   Well, he likes and respects me, but this is too much. He tells me he can't have a traitor working for him.

Dr. G.   What does he do?

Ivy.   He fires me.

Thomas's boss was a committed patriot. He even lost some of his better customers because they sided with the British. Even though Thomas was a responsible and diligent employee as well as a friend, he had crossed the line.

Dr. G.   What will you do now?

Ivy.   First, I'm going home to tell Abigale, and then I have to see Katherine.

Thomas explained most of his situation to Abigale, leaving out, of course, the part concerning Katherine and the espionage activities. He simply told her that his former boss had been unreasonable, accusing anyone who remained neutral of being a traitor.

Dr. G.   Did Abigale try to talk to your ex-boss about getting your job back?

Ivy.   She did suggest that, but I convinced her that it wouldn't do any good, so she let it go.

Dr. G.   Do you think she suspects your involvement with Katherine and these activities?

Ivy.   I really don't know. Abigale is very supportive of everything I do. Even if she just suspected my affair with Katherine, I know her well enough to know that she'd ignore the signs and hope I would make the right choice.

Thomas was quite correct about Abigale. She totally trusted and supported him. But as thoroughly as he read Abigale, he misjudged Katherine. He could never bring himself to realize that he was being used by this attractive and sensuous British agent.

Since he was now out of work, Katherine felt this was a perfect opportunity to get Thomas to make trips to other cities and towns. These would take him away from Abigale and Williamsburg for days at a time.

Dr. G.   What did you decide to do?

Ivy.   I told Abigale that I had an employment opportunity that would mean a lot of traveling. She agreed that it would be best since we needed the money.

Dr. G.   Didn't she ask you who you would be working for and what you would be doing?

Ivy.   I told her it was related to some of the business contacts I made when I worked at the print shop. She seemed satisfied with that explanation and supported my decision.

Katherine spent a lot of time with Thomas now. He simply told Abigale that he was being trained for his new job. Katherine seduced him over and over again. She made Thomas dependent upon her, and he took her bait. She briefed him about his various missions, which became more and more dangerous.

Dr. G.   Doesn't the danger of these missions disturb you?

> Ivy.   I try not to think of it. After all, I am being
>   well paid, and Katherine spends more
>   time with me when I agree to go.

By this time, Abigale was finally becoming suspicious about
the relationship between Katherine and Thomas. Instead of
expressing his usual tender and loving attitude, he was frequently
cold and distant. Still, Abigale refused to confront him. She stood
by her man and continued to support him.

I then progressed Thomas forward to the result of these
missions.

> Ivy.   It's unbelievable!

> Dr. G. What is?

> Ivy.   This is serious stuff. I mean, at first it was al-
>   most easy. These trips were routine, and I
>   enjoyed the ride.

> Dr. G. And now?

> Ivy.   I almost got killed on this last trip. These
>   Army types knew when to expect me and
>   ambushed me last night.

By "Army types," Thomas was referring to members of the
Colonial Army. Although they lacked uniforms and were un-
trained, this rag-tag group of men was deadly serious about the
war and suspected Thomas from his previous trips. When they
nearly killed him on this last mission, it had a sobering effect.

> Dr. G. What will you do about this?

> Ivy.   I'm quitting. It's just not worth it. No matter
>   how much money they pay me, it just isn't
>   worth giving up my life.

> Dr. G. Did you tell Katherine about your plans to
>   leave her employ?

Ivy.   Not yet, but I will tomorrow.

I suspected that this would not be a pleasant conversation. Katherine did not seem the type of person who would easily take no for an answer.

Dr. G.   What happened when you told Katherine that you were quitting? How did she take the news?

Ivy.   She went crazy. It was like talking to a complete stranger. She cursed me and threatened me.

Dr. G.   How did she threaten you?

Ivy.   She said she would tell Abigale about us and then turn me in to the authorities for spying.

Dr. G.   What are you going to do?

Ivy.   I told her she could do what she wants. I would tell Abigale everything tonight, and if they turned me in, I would cooperate with the Army and help them arrest all of Katherine's people.

This was the last thing Katherine wanted to hear. The next thing Thomas knew she took a gun out of a drawer and nearly got off a shot at him. Thomas struck her arm at the last second and knocked her unconscious. He took her gun and headed for his home. When he arrived at home, Abigale instantly knew something was wrong. Thomas looked a mess and had a gun in his pocket. He sat her down and explained everything to her.

Dr. G.   How did she take the news?

Ivy.   Not well. She wasn't angry at me, just disappointed. Abigale was frightened that I would be killed. She knows what happens to people who are caught spying. Taking sides with the English is one thing, but spying—that is treason.

Dr. G. What are you going to do?

Ivy. I really have no choice. I'm going to go to the Army and tell them all I know.

As it turned out, luck was not on Thomas's side. When Katherine regained consciousness, she was furious. All she could think of was revenge. She wanted to get even with Thomas if it was the last thing she did. But time was not on her side, either. Shortly after she left to meet with her fellow agents, she was arrested. Upon interrogation, she told the Army about Thomas, claiming he was the leader of this spy ring. A warrant was issued for his arrest.

Thomas was unaware of these facts until later, so he was shocked when the Army arrested him. He was imprisoned and never saw Katherine again. I progressed him forward to the outcome of the espionage charges.

Dr. G. What is going on now, Thomas?

Ivy. I feel so guilty and depressed. I let everyone down—my boss, Abigale, my country, even Katherine.

Dr. G. What is going to happen to you?

Ivy. I'm being tried for treason.

Dr. G. And if you are found guilty, what will they do to you?

Ivy. What they do to all traitors. They simply hang them from a tall tree.

Dr. G. When is your trial?

Ivy. Soon, very soon.

Thomas's trial did not go well. He was, in fact, guilty of espionage, and extenuating circumstances were not taken into account in eighteenth-century Williamsburg. Everyone testified against him, even his former boss. The fact that there was little direct evidence didn't make much difference. Hearsay evidence was admitted, and everyone knew what the verdict was going to be before the trial began.

During this most difficult time, the only bright element in Thomas's life was Abigale. She totally supported her husband. The townspeople shunned her, and life was not easy for her, but she still visited Thomas every day. She was probably the only thing keeping him sane, and he loved her for it.

Dr. G. What was the verdict?

Ivy. Guilty.

Dr. G. When are they going to hang you?

Ivy. In two days.

Dr. G. Did you ever find out what happened to Katherine and her friends?

Ivy. Yeah, they got them all. I mean they all were hung.

Dr. G. How do you feel about her now?

Ivy. Good riddance. I can't believe I let her talk me into doing all this. It was as if I didn't have a mind of my own.

Dr. G. How do you feel about Abigale?

Ivy. I love her so much. After all I did to her, all that I put her through, she still wants me. You know what she said to me when I saw her last?

Dr. G. No, what?

Ivy.   One thing she regrets about all this is that we
        never had a son. The war is all but over.
        We won and I lost. Imagine, she wanted a
        son to remind her of me. (Patient begins
        to cry in trance.) I wish I could make it up
        to her.

Thomas was hung two days later. Abigale couldn't bear to
watch him die. She left town shortly after he was buried.

From the superconscious mind level, I discovered that, not
surprisingly, Katherine is John and Abigale is Dave. Thomas's
boss is Ivy's current-life sister. This life is especially significant in
that, although it is yet another past life as a male, it represents
the closest love bond between Ivy and Dave.

And the roll John played as Katherine in this past life, as we
shall see, is only too consistent with his karmic pattern.

7: A TAILOR'S TRIUMPH

Ivy's problems with John were not completely resolved when I began the next regression. She reported having seen him a few times. However, there had been no sexual involvement; Ivy was finally able to successfully reject John's advances. Still, she hadn't been able to entirely cut off the relationship. Though it's difficult to quantify progress, I would have said that she was nearing the end of therapy, about seventy-five percent of the way there. Also, her relationship with Dave was improving, and this was a good sign.

As we began the next past-life regression, I noted a new attitude of confidence in Ivy's body position and facial expression. Since her subconscious mind would know well in advance the details of any past-life experience, I interpreted this as a good omen.

Dr. G.   Where are you?

Ivy.   I am in town at the market.

Dr. G. What is your name?

Ivy.   Janie.

Dr. G. Janie, how old are you?

Ivy.   Fifteen.

Dr. G. Where do you live?

Ivy.   Ireland.

Ivy described a rural life with her parents and four brothers and sisters. Her father was a potato farmer in the year 1849. This was not a good time as Ireland was experiencing one of the worst potato famines in history.

Janie was a well-meaning youth, but times were hard. When she went into town with her father, she would steal food and sometimes clothes. She would rather not have to do this, but it was a matter of survival.

Dr. G. Does your father know what you are doing?

Ivy.   Yes, he does, but he doesn't like it.

Dr. G. Does he forbid you from this stealing?

Ivy.   No. You see, we are poor people. We are honest but we will starve if I don't do this. My father is a proud man.

So this became a pattern for Janie. Her father would take her into town, where he would look for odd jobs, but could rarely find enough work to support his family. He was too proud to steal. This was Janie's idea, purely a matter of survival.

Dr. G. Janie, tell me what you like to do with your time.

Ivy.   I like to make clothes. I can sew real good.

Dr. G. How do you get along with your brothers and sisters?

Ivy.   I have two brothers and two sisters. We fight
       sometimes but I guess we get along. It's
       real hard because we're always hungry.

Dr. G.   Why don't they come into town with you?

Ivy.   My brothers work the farm and do their
       chores. My sisters help Mom. They would
       never do what I do.

Janie was a spunky young girl. She had no inhibitions about
going after what she wanted. She didn't like stealing, but would
do what it took to eat.

I progressed Janie forward to a significant event.

Dr. G.   How old are you now?

Ivy.   Seventeen.

Dr. G.   Do you have a boyfriend?

Ivy.   Yes.

Dr. G.   Tell me about him.

Ivy.   He works down by the docks. I like him okay,
       but he's real shy and quiet.

Dr. G.   What is going on in your life these days?

Ivy.   I'm going into town later to get some food,
       and I am going to try to get some lace to
       make a fancy dress.

Janie went into town by herself this day, and after stealing
some food, she was in a fabric store about to steal some lace.

Dr. G.   Tell me what's going on now.

Ivy.   I'm so nervous. The owner of the store keeps
       looking over at me.

Dr. G.   Are you worried that he will catch you steal-
         ing?

Ivy.   Yes. I have never been caught, and I better not
         be this time.

Dr. G.   Go on. What happened?

Ivy.   The owner grabbed me as I was about to leave
         and shook me. He found the lace I stole
         and took me into his office.

Dr. G.   What is he going to do?

Ivy.   He said he was going to have me arrested.

Dr. G.   What did you do?

Ivy.   I cried and told him I would do anything if he
         would just let me go.

Dr. G.   What happened next?

Ivy.   Well, he just looked at me kind of funny. Then
         he came over to me and put his hand on
         my knee and said he would let me go if I
         let him touch me.

Dr. G.   What did you do?

Ivy.   I didn't want him touching me, but I couldn't
         let him turn me in so I said okay.

Dr. G.   What happened next?

Ivy.   He started to touch me and my skin crawled. I
         didn't like it at all.

Dr. G.   What happened then?

Ivy.   He ripped my blouse. I tried to yell, but he put
         something in my mouth.

Janie described a harrowing rape scene. The shop owner gagged Janie with fabric so she couldn't scream. Then he tore off the rest of her clothes while slapping her a number of times. Janie fought back as best she could but she was not a match for him. The shop owner eventually knocked Janie unconscious and had his way with her. When he was done, he removed the gag and told her to get dressed. He said he would have her arrested for stealing if she ever told anyone.

Janie was in shock. She didn't know what to do. When she arrived home, her father immediately questioned her.

Dr. G.   What did your father say to you?

Ivy.   He said I looked a mess and asked me what happened.

Dr. G.   What did you tell him?

Ivy.   I can't lie to my dad so I cried and told him the whole truth.

Dr. G.   What did he say?

Ivy.   I just couldn't believe it. Instead of being angry with the store owner, he was mad at me. He told me I shouldn't have tried to steal the lace.

Dr. G.   Go on.

Ivy.   I mean, it's as if he would have only been mad if I got raped because of stealing food.

Dr. G.   What actions did your father take?

Ivy.   He slapped me and told me to leave his house forever the next day.

Dr. G.   Just like that, he abandoned you?

Ivy.   Yes. I told you my father is a proud man. He never liked my stealing, but to be raped was too much for him. I'm so ashamed.

Janie didn't sleep well that night. She knew her father would never change his mind. Nobody in her family would support her so she went to see her boyfriend the next day.

Dr. G.   What are you going to do?

Ivy.   I have to leave. The only place I can go where nobody knows me and where I can find work is England.

Dr. G.   How can your boyfriend help?

Ivy.   He works on the docks. It won't be hard for him to arrange a passage to London.

And so Janie left her family and the green hills of Ireland behind as she went to London.

I progressed her forward to a time after she settled in to her new life.

Dr. G.   Where are you now?

Ivy.   I'm working as a seamstress.

Dr. G.   That sounds like a great job for you.

Ivy.   It is, but I don't like my boss.

Dr. G.   What seems to be the problem?

Ivy.   Well, I work real hard, and I'm a good seamstress. I take pride in what I do, but he is never satisfied.

Dr. G.   Tell me more about your job.

Ivy.   I work in a factory. There are many other girls who work with me.

Dr. G.   What kind of clothes do you make?

Ivy.   Nothing fancy. We just make clothes for every-
day people.

Dr. G.   What does your boss think of you?

Ivy.   He just wants me to work faster. He doesn't
care about the quality of the clothes, but
he just wants to make money.

Janie described a sweat-shop situation. Her boss Sam was
the owner of the business, something like a discount retail
operation. Sam stole designs from other stores and hired girls
like Janie for low wages to undercut his competitors' prices. He
was ruthless and impatient.

Dr. G.   Does your boss pick on you?

Ivy.   Yes, he does. The other girls tell me that he
does that to all the new girls.

Dr. G.   How are you supporting yourself?

Ivy.   I'm getting by. I live with three other girls
from the factory in an apartment. It's not
much of a place, but I have enough to eat.

It was interesting that since she moved to London, Janie's
life had actually improved. She made enough money to keep
herself well fed. Her job gave her the opportunity to obtain
material to make her own clothes.

Dr. G.   Tell me more about your boss.

Ivy.   He is always talking about money. He smokes
bad smelling cigars and curses at everyone.

Dr. G.   Is he still picking on you?

Ivy.   He picks on everyone. No matter how hard we
work, he is always complaining. There is
just no pleasing the man.

Dr. G. Do you miss your family and the boy you left behind in Ireland?

Ivy. Not really. My family threw me out. I know I can make it on my own. As far as my boy-friend is concerned, we really weren't that close. It's time I started a whole new life.

When I asked Ivy these questions, I was trying to find out who was most likely to be Dave and John, since this was her main issue, and she habitually chose to re-live lives in which Dave and John were represented.

I progressed Janie forward to an event she considered significant.

Dr. G. What is happening at this time?

Ivy. There was so much excitement at work today.

Dr. G. What happened?

Ivy. My boss Sam steals other people's designs and makes them cheaper. Today one of the tai-lors Sam stole designs from came into the factory.

Dr. G. What did he do?

Ivy. He was so mad at Sam. He threatened Sam if he ever again stole one of his designs.

Dr. G. What did Sam do?

Ivy. Sam just puffed on his cigar and wiped his forehead. He was really sweating. I loved every minute of it.

Janie was very impressed with this aggressive young tailor, named Lloyd, who owned a small shop downtown.

I moved Janie forward again.

Dr. G. What are you up to now?

Ivy. I asked one of the girls where Lloyd's shop was, and then I went there to see him.

Dr. G. For what purpose?

Ivy. Anyone who can do what he did to Sam is someone I want to meet.

Dr. G. What happened when you went to his shop?

Ivy. It was strange. I liked him instantly and he liked me.

Dr. G. Go on.

Ivy. Lloyd is handsome, and he is a lot like me. We both go after what we want and don't care what anybody else says or thinks.

Dr. G. What did he say to you?

Ivy. Lloyd asked me to dine with him and I accepted.

Janie and Lloyd began keeping company. Lloyd was a well-bred, honest and hardworking tailor. He loved his work and had a wide variety of interests that fascinated Janie and opened up a whole new world for her.

Dr. G. It sounds like you have a new boyfriend.

Ivy. Oh, yes, he's wonderful. He takes me to the theater and the park. I love being with him.

Dr. G. How are things at work?

Ivy. Sam is on my back again. He found out about me seeing Lloyd and got so mad that he almost swallowed his cigar.

Dr. G. Why does he care who you date?

Ivy.   Lloyd is his competitor. Sam doesn't like to lose. He is afraid to steal any more of Lloyd's designs, and my seeing Lloyd reminds Sam of his failure.

Dr. G. But it's your life.

Ivy.   I know, but Sam can do a lot of things to make life hard for me.

Dr. G. So, you're afraid he will fire you?

Ivy.   Yes. This job does pay my bills, and there aren't that many jobs I can get where I can sew.

Janie was in a very delicate situation. She needed her job but wanted to keep seeing Lloyd. As time went by, she worked this out by lying to Sam. She told him that she had broken up with Lloyd, and the other girls supported her.

I moved Janie forward in time to check in on her progress.

Dr. G. Janie, what have you been up to?

Ivy.   I'm seeing a lot more of Lloyd. He has such big plans.

Dr. G. What do you mean?

Ivy.   He wants to expand his shop to cater to a better class of customers.

Dr. G. I mean, his plans for you.

Ivy.   Oh, silly me. Lloyd hasn't had much experience with girls. He is a little awkward but I know he likes me.

During the next few months things progressed rapidly in Janie's life. Her relationship with Lloyd grew by leaps and bounds. Lloyd was as good as his word and expanded his shop. His work was becoming well known, and his customer base increased both in quality and quantity. The problem was that he had so much work to do, he couldn't handle all of it.

Dr. G.   How are things between you and Lloyd?

Ivy.   Okay, I guess. Poor Lloyd is working so hard these days that I hardly see him.

Dr. G.   Is this straining your relationship?

Ivy.   Not really. I understand and support him for what he is trying to do.

Dr. G.   How is your job coming along?

Ivy.   Something strange happened this week, and I don't know what to do about it.

Dr. G.   What is it?

Ivy.   Sam came up to me and touched my back while I was working.

Dr. G.   Go on.

Ivy.   It was unpleasant. For a moment, I felt I was back in Ireland being touched by that horrible man.

Dr. G.   What happened next?

Ivy.   I turned around and grabbed his hand and dug my nails in.

Dr. G.   What did Sam do then?

Ivy.   He screamed and told me he would break my arm if I ever did that again. He has never spoken that way to me before.

Dr. G.   Are you going to tell Lloyd about this?

Ivy.   No, I'm afraid to. If I told him, I don't know what he'd do. Lloyd hates Sam. He just

might kill Sam, and as much as I hate Sam,
I don't want his blood on my conscience.

So Janie kept quiet about the incident, and Sam never approached her again in the factory, though he occasionally leered at her. This made her very uncomfortable, but she didn't feel she could complain about the way someone looked at her.

Later that evening, something strange happened.

Dr. G.   What is it, Janie?

Ivy.   My roommates received an invitation to dinner at a hotel and they left.

Dr. G.   Who sent this invitation?

Ivy.   That is just it. It was unsigned.

Dr. G.   What are you doing now?

Ivy.   I'm going to go to bed early.

Such was not to be the case. Shortly thereafter she heard a knock at the door. A man's voice said he was from the police and needed to talk to her about her roommates. He said there had been an accident at the hotel they went to earlier.

Dr. G.   What did you do next?

Ivy.   I opened the door to let the policeman in, and I couldn't believe it.

Dr. G.   What was it?

Ivy.   It was Sam. He was the one who sent the invitations. He just wanted me to be alone tonight.

Dr. G.   What about your roommates?

Ivy.   That was a lie. They are all okay. It's me that I am worried about.

Janie was quite correct to be in fear of the situation. Sam locked the door behind him and proceeded to beat and rape her. She had no idea what motivated him to commit such a brutal act but the answer came after he finished with her.

Dr. G. Are you all right?

Ivy. No, I'm a mess.

Dr. G. Why did he do this?

Ivy. Sam is a sick man. He told me he followed me a couple of times and saw me with Lloyd. It upset him that I lied to him, and he has wanted me for a long time anyway, so he concocted this plan to get rid of my room-mates and rape me tonight.

Dr. G. What will you do?

Ivy. I'm not going back to his factory, that's for sure. Tomorrow I will see Lloyd, and I'm going to tell him what happened.

Janie did just that. When she told Lloyd the details, he saw red. All he could think of was to punish Sam. Later that night Lloyd went to Sam's home and beat him severely. Sam was black and blue and lucky to be alive.

Dr. G. What happened after Lloyd beat up Sam?

Ivy. He proposed to me. Lloyd told me he was going to propose to me soon anyway, but he wanted to marry me now.

Dr. G. What did you say to him?

Ivy. I accepted, of course.

Janie and Lloyd were married. She invited a number of the girls she used to work with at Sam's factory. Sam hated both of them now, but there was nothing he could do.

I progressed Janie forward again.

> Dr. G. What has transpired since I last spoke to you?
>
> Ivy. Everything is wonderful. Lloyd and I work together in his shop. We got so busy that we needed extra seamstresses, so I suggested he hire some of my friends from Sam's factory.
>
> Dr. G. How did that work out?
>
> Ivy. Great! The girls couldn't wait to quit working for Sam. They got raises to work for us, and they just love it.
>
> Dr. G. That must not have made Sam happy.
>
> Ivy. Sam is furious. I still see some of the girls who work for him, and he is just impossible. He told them that if anyone so much as mentions my name, he will fire them right on the spot.

As the months went by, Janie's life with Lloyd became more and more fulfilling. Lloyd's shop did very well, and she put Sam out of her mind. Unfortunately, Sam didn't reciprocate. His business began to suffer. He found it difficult to replace the girls who went to work for Lloyd. Sam became obsessed with Janie. He blamed her for all of his troubles and mentally plotted her destruction.

Janie heard of Sam's paranoia through some of her old friends who still worked for him, but she disregarded it and went on with her life.

> Dr. G. What is going on at this time?
>
> Ivy. I've got wonderful news. I'm pregnant!
>
> Dr. G. Congratulations!

Ivy.   Thank you. Lloyd and I are so happy. The busi-
         ness is going well, and my friends are work-
         ing for us, so it is just a pleasure to go to
         work every day. I never thought life could
         be like this.

Indeed, this was quite a change from that ragged girl from
Ireland. Janie had come a long way, mostly through her own
efforts. She greatly assisted Lloyd in making their shop a success,
and now she was pregnant with their child.

I moved Janie forward to a significant event.

Dr. G.   Where are you now?

Ivy.   I'm about to lock up the shop.

Dr. G.   Go on.

Ivy.   There's a man in front of the shop, just stand-
         ing there.

Dr. G.   Do you know who he is?

Ivy.   No. All I can see is his back.

Dr. G.   Where is Lloyd?

Ivy.   He is in the back, putting some material away.

Dr. G.   What happens next?

Ivy.   The man comes into the shop, and he is point-
         ing a gun at me. Oh, my God, it's Sam!

Dr. G.   What does he want?

Ivy.   He says he is going to kill me because I'm re-
         sponsible for his business's failing.

Dr. G.   What do you do?

Ivy.   I can't move. I'm frightened. He's going to
         pull the trigger.

We all know that sometimes in an emergency everything seems to move in slow motion. Death scenes in past lives are often described in a very similar way. What happened next appeared to Janie to occur in slow motion. Lloyd came in from the storeroom and there was a struggle. He shot Sam in the chest, and he died instantly.

The police report cleared Lloyd of any wrongdoing. It was obviously a case of self-defense. So many people came forward to testify against Sam that the police had a hard time keeping up with them. So, finally, the protagonist of one of Ivy's past lives, Janie, lived happily ever after with her mate, Lloyd.

There are several significant things about this life. Ivy's superconscious mind informed me that Lloyd is Dave, and Sam is John, as we might have suspected. But in this life Dave bested John and lived to tell about it. More importantly, Ivy actually lived out her life in peace; this life represented her ideal frequency, to which it was my therapeutic goal to program her. A more detailed explanation of parallel frequencies can be found in *Past Lives–Future Lives* (Chapter 22).

8: THE WORST OF TIMES

Skeptics about past-life regression like to raise issues concerning dates in an attempt to invalidate the past life by showing how the date of birth in one life overlapped part of another life—the assumption is that it's impossible for one soul to have occupied both bodies. Nothing could be farther from the truth than this conception of time, however.

Quantum physics has now shown that there are an infinite number of parallel universes. (I refer you to the bibliography and the excellent books by Fred Allan Wolf, a quantum physicist, for a more detailed explanation.) In parallel universes, or frequencies, apparent simultaneity actually occurs in different time continuums which only appear to overlap. Lives on the same frequency never overlap. Skeptics, especially those who pride themselves on scientific rationalism, must come to terms with the fact that fields such as advanced physics and nonlinear dynamics are revealing daily that concepts formerly ridiculed as "metaphysical"—multidimensionality, simultaneity, even reincarnation and karma—are now the province of hard science.

In the life we are about to detail, Ivy was born right after her death as Thomas in Williamsburg and died just prior to her birth as Doris in Philadelphia, related in Chapter 10. In these cases, she remained on the same frequency. However, you will note that these dates overlap Ivy's life as a Polish pianist, which occurred on a completely different frequency.

Ivy was excited, as usual, about beginning a new exploration into a past life. She didn't have many questions about the previous session and wanted to get right on with it.

Dr. G. Where are you?

Ivy.   I'm at home with my father.

Dr. G. What is your name?

Ivy.   Monique.

Dr. G. Tell me about yourself.

Ivy.   I like to make clothes. We don't have much money, so it's a way I can help out.

Dr. G. Tell me about your parents.

Ivy.   My mother died when I was a child, and I don't have any brothers or sisters. Actually, I did have a baby brother, but he died a few months after he was born.

Dr. G. Tell me about your father.

Ivy.   He works in a shop in the city. He doesn't make much money, and he is sad most of the time.

Monique lived in Paris, and in the 1790's she was a teenager. Her father apparently suffered from clinical depression. The combination of the death of Monique's mother, the death of a baby son, and the difficult times of the French Revolution were overwhelming for him. He drank too much and hated the world. For him, "it was the worst of times."

Dr. G.   What do you and your dad talk about?

Ivy.   Oh, he likes to talk about politics, but I'm not interested in that.

Remember, Ivy, as Thomas, was hung for political intrigue during the American Revolution. Apparently her subconscious mind did not need another lifetime as a political activist.

Dr. G.   What does he say about politics?

Ivy.   Most of the people he knows talk about how much they hated the King, but Dad doesn't like change. He just wants things to settle down and stay the way they are.

Dr. G.   Is he supportive of the monarchy?

Ivy.   I don't know. He just didn't like it when they beheaded the King and Queen. All he really cares about is paying his bills and providing for us.

I progressed Monique forward to a significant event.

Dr. G.   What is going on at this time?

Ivy.   My dad came home from the inn and he is in bad shape.

Dr. G.   What happened?

Ivy.   He got into a fight with some men about politics.

Dr. G.   What was the issue?

> Ivy.   Well, it seems these men were bragging about how they were at the execution of the King and Queen and many other people.
>
> Dr. G. So what did your father say?
>
> Ivy.   He told them they should not be so concerned about who runs the country but should do something about trying to improve life in the city.
>
> Dr. G. Then what?
>
> Ivy.   Then these men dragged my dad out of the inn and beat him up.

In these difficult times, discussions of politics did not bring out the best in the citizens of Paris, especially if they raised the volatile issue of support for the old monarchy. I moved Monique forward again.

> Dr. G. What is going on now, Monique?
>
> Ivy.   (Crying in trance.) I feel so ashamed. I'm a bad girl.
>
> Dr. G. What happened?
>
> Ivy.   It's my dad. He got drunk and raped me.
>
> Dr. G. When did this happen?
>
> Ivy.   A few hours ago. I wish I were dead!

Monique was shaken. Her father had come home drunk on many prior occasions. But this time things were different. He was thinking of his late wife and how much he missed her. Monique had just taken a bath and was getting dressed when he came in. Monique was an attractive teenager, and this must have been too much for him in his inebriated state.

> Dr. G. What will you do now?

Ivy.   I left home and rented a room in a different part of the city.

Dr. G.   How will you support yourself?

Ivy.   Working as a server, like a waitress. I got a job working in a rundown inn. It's not great but it will support me.

During the next year, Monique tried to get her life in order. She had no contact with her father, whom she now loathed. Once in a while she would hear about him through some friends from her old neighborhood.

Dr. G.   How are things going?

Ivy.   Not well.

Dr. G.   In what way?

Ivy.   I'm having a hard time getting by. I just can't make enough money at the inn.

Dr. G.   Have you thought of asking your father for some money?

Ivy.   I will never speak to that man. It's out of the question.

I moved Monique forward to a time when this situation would be resolved.

Dr. G.   Where are you now?

Ivy.   I'm working at the inn and talking to Pierre.

Dr. G.   Who is Pierre?

Ivy.   He is the cook and a nice man.

Dr. G.   Is he your boyfriend?

Ivy.   No, he is just a friend, but I like him.

Dr. G.   What about your financial situation?

Ivy.   One of my new regular customers is a man by
        the name of Paul.

Dr. G. Go on.

Ivy.   Paul asks me a lot of questions about my life.

Dr. G. Does he want to date you?

Ivy.   Not as such. He offers to pay me money if I
        sleep with him.

Dr. G. How do you respond to that idea?

Ivy.   I slapped him in his face when he first sug-
        gested it.

Dr. G. And now?

Ivy.   I don't know. He seems okay, but I have never
        done that before.

Dr. G. Are you a virgin?

Ivy.   No, but anytime I have slept with a man it was
        because I wanted to. I have never sold my-
        self.

During the next few weeks Monique took a very important
step in her young life. She decided to take Paul up on his offer
as a matter of survival. She had far too much pride to ask her
father for money. This seemed her only way out.

Dr. G. Monique, what is happening now?

Ivy.   I slept with Paul for money.

Dr. G. How do you feel about it?

Ivy.   I'm not proud of myself, but it wasn't that bad.
        Paul is not an unattractive man, and he is
        a good lover.

Monique slept with Paul a few more times before she was presented with a most unexpected offer.

Dr. G.   What did Paul say to you?

Ivy.   He wants me to be one of his "girls".

Dr. G.   What do you mean by "one of his girls"?

Ivy.   I misjudged Paul. I thought he was just a shy man who was lonely and looking for the company of a woman.

Dr. G.   And now?

Ivy.   He is a pimp. He wants me to be a prostitute for him. I'm supposed to sleep with any man he says.

Dr. G.   What did you decide to do?

Ivy.   I thought about it and said yes.

Dr. G.   Why?

Ivy.   I am terrible at my job. I mix up orders and break dishes far more than anyone else. I just know that my boss will fire me one of these days.

Dr. G.   Anything else?

Ivy.   Yes, I find myself strangely attracted to Paul. I don't know how to explain it other than to say I can't seem to say no to him.

Monique quit her job at the inn and moved in with Paul. She became one of his prostitutes. He had six or seven other women working for him. Monique was falling in love with Paul and would literally do anything he asked.

Dr. G.   Do you enjoy your work?

Ivy.   Yes and no. I do enjoy sex but not with some of the men Paul sends me with.

Dr. G.   How does Paul treat you?

Ivy.   That's another problem.

Dr. G.   In what way?

Ivy.   Paul has these other girls and sometimes he sleeps with them.

Dr. G.   How does that affect you?

Ivy.   How do you think it does? I don't like it at all, not one bit.

Dr. G.   Do you confront him about this?

Ivy.   I tried once and he hit me.

Dr. G.   He hit you?

Ivy.   Yes, he hit me. He hits me a lot. I never know what he is going to do when I see him.

Dr. G.   Have you thought of leaving him?

Ivy.   Yes, but I can't.

Dr. G.   Why not?

Ivy.   For two reasons. I have no place to go and no money.

Dr. G.   But I thought that you are pretty active as a prostitute.

Ivy.   I do see a lot of men but you don't understand.

Dr. G.   Please explain.

Ivy.   All of the money I get from these men I give to Paul. He provides me with clothes and other needs, but I don't get much money

Ivy. for myself. If I leave him, I have nothing
but the clothes on my back.

Dr. G. And the other reason?

Ivy. The other reason is that I'm strangely attracted to Paul. I don't know what it is, but
no matter how mean he is to me, I just
can't leave him.

This is a rather typical profile of a prostitute. Frequently
they are victims of incest during their childhood or adolescence,
grow up expecting to be victimized, and often become involved
with abusive men. It is not a pretty life. Monique seemed to accept
her fate.

Dr. G. You seem somewhat upset. What has happened?

Ivy. It's my father; he's dead.

Dr. G. What happened?

Ivy. I heard from some friends from the old neighborhood that he was murdered by a group
called Jacobins.

Dr. G. How do you feel about this?

Ivy. You know, I really don't care anymore. I have
my own problems. He got what he de-
served. He raped me, and I hate him for
that. He probably picked a fight with the
wrong people at the wrong time.

It was as if Monique was relieved by this news. She wasn't
totally cold to the idea of her father's death, but it did make her
life simpler. In the past she would occasionally hear about her
father, and this would cause flashback memories of the night he
raped her. In psychotherapy, we refer to this as post-traumatic
stress disorder (PTSD). PTSD flashbacks sometimes take the

form of nightmares. Monique did experience terror dreams, but Paul was such a sound sleeper that he never knew of them. The way Monique described him, he probably wouldn't have shown much concern, anyway.

Dr. G.   Do you ever see anyone other than Paul?

Ivy.   You mean another man?

Dr. G.   Yes.

Ivy.   Well, I still see Pierre.

Dr. G.   Tell me more about your relationship with him.

Ivy.   When I worked at the inn, I made many mistakes. I told you that I broke dishes and mixed things up.

Dr. G.   Yes, you mentioned that before.

Ivy.   Some of the other employees made fun of me. The owner yelled at me all the time. It was my first job, and I didn't know what I was doing.

Dr. G.   And Pierre?

Ivy.   Pierre was different. He didn't laugh at me. He was always so kind and patient with me. It was easy to talk with him.

Dr. G.   And when you quit the inn, did you stop seeing Pierre?

Ivy.   For a while I didn't see him. Then, when Paul started treating me badly, I needed someone to talk to, so I started going back to the inn.

Dr. G.   Please continue.

Ivy.   This time I was a customer and nobody laughed at me.

Dr. G.   Did Paul know you were doing this?

Ivy.   No. I would never tell him about Pierre. Paul has a terrible temper.

Dr. G.   But since you met Paul at the inn, aren't you afraid he will see you there with Pierre?

Ivy.   The only reason Paul ate there in the first place was because of me.

Dr. G.   I don't understand. How did he know you worked there?

Ivy.   Paul saw me on the street walking to work. He simply followed me into the inn, and when he saw me working, he made sure to sit at one of my tables.

Dr. G.   How did you find all this out?

Ivy.   Paul told me so himself. He had the nerve to brag about it one night when we were in bed.

Dr. G.   Didn't that bother you?

Ivy.   Yes, it did, but no matter what he does, I just can't stay mad at him. I just don't know how to explain it.

Monique may not have understood it, but I did. It was becoming obvious to me that Paul was John. Her karmic ties with him from previous lives were so strong as to cloud her judgment. It was the same sadomasochistic relationship that had persisted through the centuries.

Dr. G.   Tell me more about Pierre.

Ivy.   I always liked him. In a way, I was attracted to him but not because of his looks. Pierre is about ten years older than me and somewhat overweight. He is a wonderful person, and I didn't know anyone I could talk to about Paul.

Dr. G. What has changed your relationship with Pierre?

Ivy.   I never saw him outside the inn, mostly because he was too shy.

Dr. G. And now?

Ivy.   Lately, I have been very lonely. Paul is rarely at home. We argue a lot, and he spends most of his nights with one of his other prostitutes.

Dr. G. Go on.

Ivy.   So now I need someone to talk to. I don't have any real friends, just some people I knew from the old neighborhood. I don't even see them very often.

Dr. G. So Pierre filled this need in you?

Ivy.   Yes, that's exactly it. Pierre seems to really understand me. All of the other men I have ever known just want to sleep with me. Pierre is different.

Dr. G. And your feelings towards him. Aren't they different, also?

Ivy.   Yes, they are. I can't explain it, but I feel this bond between us. He is very special.

Dr. G. Do you want to be with Pierre in other ways?

Ivy.   I don't know. Right now, all I know is that I
        am a whore. I don't like what I do, and I'm
        living with a man who beats me, controls
        me, and whom I just can't seem to leave. I
        am in a real mess.

Monique was becoming more and more depressed. The fact
that her father had suffered from major depression didn't improve her prognosis. (There is some evidence of genetic predisposition to such depression.) Monique's hopelessness and
helplessness, coupled with occasional bouts of insomnia, didn't
paint a pleasant picture. She was drifting through life with no
direction, and she was miserable.

I progressed Monique forward to a significant event in her
relationship with Paul.

Dr. G.   What's going on now?

Ivy.   Paul is becoming impossible to live with.

Dr. G.   What has he done now?

Ivy.   He beats me more often. He won't even sleep
          with me. I am afraid he is going to throw
          me out.

Dr. G.   Does he threaten to do that?

Ivy.   Not yet, but he will.

Dr. G.   How do you know that?

Ivy.   I spoke with one of his other "girls". She has
          known him for a long time. She tells me
          that this is his pattern. After he tires of a
          girl he lives with, he works her harder and
          harder. Then he stops sleeping with her
          and spends most of his time with the other
          girls. Then he gets rid of her. That is ex-
          actly what is happening to me.

Monique was in a very difficult position. She had absolutely no control over her life and was at the mercy of Paul. The only emotional support system she had was Pierre. But she couldn't just run to Pierre every time she had a problem without Paul finding out. Monique was not about to lose the man she was so strangely drawn to. She also feared for Pierre. Paul had shown some very violent traits, and she was afraid he might discover her friendship with Pierre.

Dr. G.   Why are you so concerned about Paul finding out about Pierre?

Ivy.   One of Paul's girls told me a story that really frightened me.

Dr. G.   What was that?

Ivy.   A few years ago a man tried to take one of Paul's girls from him. Paul did not know this man very well, and he really didn't care much for the girl, either.

Dr. G.   What happened?

Ivy.   Paul went crazy. He is very possessive over his girls. They got into an argument and Paul stabbed him to death.

Dr. G.   I see the reason for your concern.

Ivy.   Paul has many knives in his place. It's almost a collection. He always carries at least one with him at all times. I'm only realizing how dangerous he really is.

Dr. G.   Does this convince you that you should leave him, and the sooner, the better?

Ivy.   I know I should but I can't. My heart just isn't in it. I feel so tired and defeated. Paul works me so hard that I'm exhausted.

The situation was getting out of hand. Monique was in real danger now but just didn't have the motivation or the courage to do something about it.

I moved her forward to a significant event.

Dr. G. What has happened since I last spoke with you?

Ivy. Pierre was very concerned about me. The last time I saw him, I looked a mess. He also saw how depressed I was.

Dr. G. What did he say to you?

Ivy. He knew my situation, and he offered to let me stay with him. He said I wouldn't have to sleep with him. He is so sweet.

Dr. G. Did you accept his offer?

Ivy. I told him I would think about it. I did. I thought about it a lot. It was not just getting away from Paul but being with the only person in the city that I could really talk to and who cared about me. Pierre is the only man who ever respected me. To the rest of the world, I'm just a whore.

Dr. G. Please continue.

Ivy. I really seriously considered leaving Paul, but I got so depressed, I just did nothing. I couldn't even work.

Dr. G. What did Paul do?

Ivy. Paul let me alone when he saw me this way. He knew no man wants a depressed whore.

Dr. G. What about Pierre?

Ivy.   Since it had been a while since I came to see him, Pierre came over here.

Dr. G.   What happened?

Ivy.   We had a nice long talk but Paul saw him leaving and became very angry with me.

Dr. G.   What did he say to you?

Ivy.   He accused me of holding out on him. Can you believe that? He actually accused me of sleeping with Pierre. But it wasn't sex that bothered him, it was the money.

Dr. G.   What money?

Ivy.   Paul accused me of accepting money from Pierre for sex and hiding it from him.

Dr. G.   Then what?

Ivy.   Then Paul beat me and told me he was going to "take care" of Pierre.

Dr. G.   What did you do?

Ivy.   I couldn't do anything. Paul beat me up so badly that I was unconscious and locked me in my room.

This was a difficult time for Monique. Her only friend was probably in mortal danger, and there was nothing she could do about it.

I moved her forward to the resolution of this matter.

Dr. G.   What happened?

Ivy.   I can't go on. It's too late for me.

Dr. G.   What is, Monique? What has happened?

Ivy.   It's Paul. He finally did it. He followed Pierre
to the inn and picked a fight with him.
Pierre doesn't like to fight so Paul became
more aggressive.

Dr. G.   Go on.

Ivy.   Pierre turned his back to leave, and that was
his big mistake.

Dr. G.   What did Paul do?

Ivy.   Paul stabbed Pierre in the back. He killed
Pierre, the only man who really cared
about me.

Dr. G.   What will you do now?

Ivy.   I have nothing to live for. Paul is probably going to kill me, so I'll save him the trouble.

Monique took one of Paul's knives and slashed her wrists.
She made a ritual of it. First, she drew herself a bath and then
poured herself some wine. She thought of her father, her job at
the inn, her relationship with Paul, her days as a common
streetwalker—all the failures in her life. It was just too much. She
had been in a major depressive episode, and Pierre's death
pushed her over the edge.

From the superconscious mind level, I identified the people
in her life. Her father was an ex-boyfriend in her current life as
Ivy. Paul, as expected, was John, and Pierre was Dave.

The karmic triangle was becoming more intesnse with each
succeeding life. In this case Dave was totally supportive of Ivy
without being her lover. John was his usual jealous and violent
self; his actions came as no surprise. And Ivy's capacity for
victimization seemed to know no bounds.

I later discovered this interesting historical note in *The
Outline of History* (757–758, 762, 767–768):

These Jacobins were the equivalents of the American radicals, men with untrammeled advanced ideas. Their strength lay in the fact that they were unencumbered...poor men with nothing to lose.... Robespierre was a needy but clever young lawyer from Arras whose most precious possession was his faith in Rousseau. Such was the quality of most of the leaders of the Jacobin party. They were men of no property—untethered men. They were more dissociated and more elemental, therefore, than any other party; and they were ready to push the ideas of freedom and equality to a logical extremity. Their standards of patriotic virtue were high and harsh. There was something inhuman even in their humanitarian zeal. They saw without humor the disposition of the moderates to ease things down....

And while in America the formulae of eighteenth-century democracy were on the whole stimulating and helpful ... in France, these formulae made a very heady and dangerous mixture for the town populations, because considerable parts of the towns of France were slums full of dispossessed, demoralized, degraded, and bitter-spirited people. The Parisian crowd was in a particularly desperate and dangerous state.... the city was full of unemployed and angry people.

The National Convention met on September 21, 1792, and immediately proclaimed a republic. The trial and execution of the King followed with a sort of logical necessity upon these things. Louis was beheaded in January 1793.... The story of the Republic after the summer of 1794 becomes a tangled story of political groups aiming at everything from a radical republic to a royalist reaction....There was a series of insurrections of the Jacobins and the royalists: there seems to have been what we should call nowadays a hooligan class in Paris which was quite ready to turn out to fight and loot on either side.... The last, most threatening revolt of all, in October 1795, was suppressed with great skill and decision by a rising young general, Napoleon Bonaparte.

Monique's birth was sometime around 1780 and her death around 1798. The historical data once again gives suggestive evidence to confirm Ivy's past-life descriptions.

9: ROMAN HOLOCAUST

Ivy was regressed in my office a total of 46 times. Though at least 20 of these lives shed some light on elements of the fatal triangle played out in the life of Grace Doze, I have restricted my narrations in this book to those lives which graphically illustrate different aspects of the karmic dynamics involved. While it is only natural to look for a beginning to such a dramatic pattern of intersecting emotions, as I have mentioned, time and karma just don't work that way. The conventions of linear causation we all use to explain our lives on a day-to-day basis are really an illusion, a construct of the simplistic Newtonian model of the universe Western Civilization has accepted by consensus.

Nevertheless, it is interesting to observe an "earlier" stage of the relationship between these souls as revealed in one of the chronologically earliest of Ivy's past lives, which took place in ancient Rome. When I do enough past-life regressions on the same patient, lives during the great ancient civilizations are often uncovered.

Ivy began this particular past-life regression as she had the others we had done. She didn't know in advance that she was about to expose another aspect of her karmic relationship with John.

> Dr. G. Where are you at this time?
>
> Ivy.   I'm in my shop.
>
> Dr. G. What do you do?
>
> Ivy.   I make pottery, decorative pottery.
>
> Dr. G. You seem especially proud of what you do.
>
> Ivy.   I am. My work is beautiful, and many wealthy people in Rome come to my shop to buy it, even if they don't really appreciate what they are getting.
>
> Dr. G. What do people call you?
>
> Ivy.   I am Josephus.

In this life Ivy was a craftsman named Josephus, about twenty-five years old, who owned a specialty pottery shop in Rome catering to the wealthy, sometime in the first century AD. She displayed a confident, almost elitist attitude in her responses to my questions. Never before had she presented herself in this manner. She usually came across as an excited teenager or an insecure young adult.

Josephus did not care much for the Romans, especially the rich Romans. As I continued with my questioning, I uncovered some striking facts.

> Dr. G. Josephus, you don't seem to like your fellow citizens much.
>
> Ivy.   I judge people by who they are, not how much money they have or who they know.
>
> Dr. G. What is it about the Romans you don't like?

Ivy.   Everything. They are greedy, uneducated, superficial and tasteless.

Dr. G. Then why do you live and work here?

Ivy.   Art is my life. I have to sell my work, and Rome is the best market for what I do. Most rural people couldn't afford my work, so I sell it to these pigs.

Dr. G. Is there any other reason why you dislike the Romans so much?

Ivy.   They are pagans, brutal pagans.

Dr. G. And you?

Ivy.   I am a Christian.

Dr. G. Isn't this a dangerous place for you to be as a Christian?

Ivy.   Most definitely. I cannot practice my religious beliefs openly. It is not fair.

Dr. G. Have any of your friends suffered as a result of their religious convictions?

Ivy.   Yes. I have lost some of my family due to these barbarians.

Dr. G. Aren't you concerned for your own safety?

Ivy.   Yes, but it is easy to outsmart these Romans. We conduct our services in secret and have for many years.

So Josephus had good reason to hate the Romans. They were literally crucifying his fellow Christians, or throwing them to the lions in the Coliseum. In addition, he felt superior to his customers due to his education and refined background. Josephus had chosen a line of work reflecting his fine tastes, making decorations for wealthy dilettantes. But he was such an excellent craftsman he found it degrading to have to sell his work to an undeserving clientele.

> Dr. G. Are you married at this time?
>
> Ivy.   No. I live by myself.
>
> Dr. G. Do you have a girlfriend?
>
> Ivy.   No. I am not particularly interested in the women of Rome. They are women of low morals.
>
> Dr. G. So, what do you put your energies into?
>
> Ivy.   I have my work, which is very demanding of my time. I also have my faith in God.

The worst thing about Josephus's day was dealing with his customers. He loved making the pottery and other decorative items, but he had nothing but disdain for the Romans who bought them. His theological beliefs were an important part of his life, though he was not a religious fanatic by any means, but merely a serious Christian.

> Dr. G. What makes your pottery so valuable?
>
> Ivy.   I do many things other than pottery. All my work is beautifully detailed. Many people can pick up a piece of my work in someone's home and identify it as mine.
>
> Dr. G. Your work is that well known?
>
> Ivy.   Yes, by those who appreciate true beauty.
>
> Dr. G. Do you ever make any religious artifacts?

This question seemed to hit a nerve. Ivy just froze in my office recliner. She arched her back and gave me a look of disgust.

> Ivy.   Yes, I make pagan pieces for these fools.
>
> Dr. G. If this bothers you so much, why do it?

> Ivy.   I do what I am contracted to do. I can't afford to raise suspicions.

Josephus was no fool. He may have been vain, but he knew human nature. These were dangerous days for Christians, who were persecuted severely in Rome at that time—crucified in the public square or thrown to wild beasts in the arena. The Roman soldiers were constantly on the alert for Christians, in a situation analogous to the persecution of Jews in German-dominated Europe in the 1930's and 1940's.

The last thing Josephus wanted to do was raise suspicions about himself or call attention to his background. Refusing to create statues and other items honoring the pagan gods of the Romans was not just bad business, it could easily arouse speculation as to Josephus's religious orientation. No loyal pagan Roman artist and sculptor would refuse such a request.

I moved Josephus forward by a few years.

> Dr. G.   Where are you now?
>
> Ivy.   I'm attending a service.
>
> Dr. G.   Did you come here by yourself?
>
> Ivy.   No, I came with Laramus.

Josephus was still a single man. Laramus was a fellow Christian and his best friend. They went to the theater together and shared common ideologies. The Christian services were held in secret, with someone always keeping a watchful eye out for Roman soldiers. Josephus, Laramus, and the others who regularly attended the religious services were careful, intelligent men. They paid attention to detail and were expert at keeping their activities secret from the Roman Army. The tales that circulated of other Christian groups being discovered and slaughtered only added to their incentive to outthink their enemy.

I continued with my questioning.

Dr. G. Do you ever have any close calls with Roman soldiers?

Ivy. No. We are a lot smarter than them. My people are very careful. I do not understand why they bother us so. We hurt no one. They are fools.

Dr. G. What kind of precautions do you take?

Ivy. We use a different location each time. The exact location isn't decided upon until shortly before the services. I then bring the items.

Dr. G. What items?

Ivy. I have made the crosses and implements that are used in our services. After each service I remove them and hide them in my shop.

I then progressed Josephus forward to an event that would be important to him.

Dr. G. What has happened since I last spoke to you?

Ivy. It's terrible. (Ivy was crying.)

Dr. G. What is it?

Ivy. The soldiers—they killed my parents and some cousins.

Dr. G. How did this happen?

Ivy. The soldiers raided one of their services. They have spies everywhere, you know. They heard about their congregation so they sent some soldiers to investigate.

Dr. G. What did they do?

Ivy.   Some who resisted were killed instantly. Others were sent to be crucified, including my parents. Two of my cousins were thrown to the lions for the entertainment of those murderous pigs.

Dr. G.   I am truly sorry to hear about your loss. Aren't you going to have to watch out for their spies?

Ivy.   Yes. We have to be extremely careful now. Many Christians, I am told, have betrayed their brothers. This is just terrible.

This was a most depressing time for Josephus. He hadn't needed any excuse to despise the Romans, and now became more aggressive about his disdain.

Dr. G.   Josephus, aren't you concerned the soldiers will trace you from your family's involvement with the church?

Ivy.   As far as these barbarians are concerned, that business is done. I am in danger as long as they continue to hunt my brother and sister Christians, but they don't know anything about me in particular.

Josephus closed his shop for a few days. He and Laramus and some others devised more detailed schemes to further protect their people from the Roman soldiers.

I progressed Josephus forward to the next meaningful event in his life.

Dr. G.   What is going on now, Josephus?

Ivy.   I came close to doing something very foolish.

Dr. G.   What was that?

Ivy.   One of my customers came into my shop and was looking at some of my pagan statues.

Dr. G.   Please go on.

Ivy.   Well, while he was deciding which one he wanted to buy, he made a comment about the recent discovery of Christian groups.

Dr. G.   Do you mean he was referring to the slaughter of your family?

Ivy.   Not specifically; there have been many churches discovered by the soldiers lately. He was bragging about how these people got what they deserved and how good the Roman army was.

Dr. G.   And you took it personally because the deaths of your parents and cousins were included in that remark?

Ivy.   Exactly. I almost lost my temper. You must understand, I have always prided myself on my sense of discipline. I cannot begin losing my self-control if I wish to survive as a Christian.

Dr. G.   Please continue.

Ivy.   To strike this idiot would have been suicidal. In addition, it would go against my religion.

Dr. G.   How did you keep your temper under control?

Ivy.   It was not easy. I held my breath and recited a prayer. I thought of our Lord, and my faith helped me to get through this.

In my experience as a past-life regression hypnotherapist, I have found that events like this often herald a serious reversal in a person's life. No doubt you have observed from Ivy's other lives that when emotional tensions begin to build, it is commonly followed by a series of karmic tests, in a snowball effect. This conversation with Josephus foreboded such a phenomenon.

Here was a very disciplined, soft-spoken man becoming obsessed with revenge—against his religious training, too, which was even more significant. I, of course, thought of Ivy's future life as the fourteenth-century friar when I did this regression. It was only Josephus's self-restraint that kept him out of trouble, at least for the time being.

I moved him forward to a meaningful event.

Dr. G. Where are you now?

Ivy. I'm at a service with our church.

Dr. G. How many others are there?

Ivy. Only a few of us. Laramus and I decided to break our regular group down into smaller numbers so that we would be safer from the army.

Dr. G. Please continue.

Ivy. It's just not the same. I don't like hiding like this, but I don't have any choice.

All of sudden, a disruption occurred. Josephus described a raid on his church by Roman soldiers.

Dr. G. What happened?

Ivy. It's the soldiers. Somehow they found out about us and they are coming.

Dr. G. Go on.

Ivy.   We are able to disperse, but I had no time to
remove my crosses and other religious sym-
bols. These barbarians will destroy my
work.

Josephus and the others escaped narrowly from this close
call. He and Laramus decided to meet the following day at
Josephus's shop to rethink their strategy for future services.

Dr. G.   What is going on now?

Ivy.   Laramus and I are meeting in my shop. He is
overwrought, angrier and more frightened
than I have ever seen him. This constant
fear is making us all lose control.

Dr. G.   Please continue.

Ivy.   We are considering our options when all of a
sudden a soldier enters the shop.

Dr. G.   What did he want?

Ivy.   He is looking for the owner. He says that someone recognized my work confiscated at the
raid.

Dr. G.   What do you do?

Ivy.   Laramus and I tell him that we are customers
waiting for the owner to return from an errand.

Dr. G.   Doesn't the soldier know what you look like?

Ivy.   Fortunately, no. This oaf shouldn't have told
us his motives before he asked for the
owner. Pagan fool!

Dr. G.   What happens next?

Ivy.   Things happen so quickly. Laramus grabbed
the soldier's sword and stabbed him without warning. I think he has killed him.

Dr. G.   Go on.

Ivy.   We took his uniform and wrapped his body up
in some cloth. We then placed him in a
cart and left my shop.

This was the beginning of a chain of events that would prove
irreversible. Josephus and Laramus dumped the soldier's body
and went to Laramus's home.

Dr. G.   Aren't you afraid the soldiers will look for
Laramus next to arrest him?

Ivy.   No, they only know about me from my work.
These fools didn't even know what I look
like. They most certainly are not going to
be knowledgeable of my friends.

Josephus was correct. In many ways, he was a loner. He did
not attend public gatherings nor did he socialize with his customers. The Romans didn't know much about him, but he was now
a fugitive. He had to use all his cunning for survival.

Dr. G.   What will you do now?

Ivy.   I don't know. I left Laramus at his place and
went off to think.

Dr. G.   Where will you go?

Ivy.   I can't go home; I can't return to my work. My
life is destroyed. Someone's going to pay
for this.

Josephus was not thinking very clearly. He was irrational and
emotional, most out of character for him. He was preoccupied
with revenge.

Dr. G. What are you going to do?

Ivy.   I am going to avenge my family.

Dr. G. How?

Ivy.   By doing to them what they did to my people—
        an eye for an eye.

Dr. G. Exactly what do you have in mind?

Ivy.   I will wear the Roman soldier's uniform. They
        don't really know what I look like, so it
        should be easy to get into the Coliseum.

Dr. G. The Coliseum? Why go there?

Ivy.   I must do it. I must.

Dr. G. But they will kill you.

Ivy.   I have a plan.

Josephus devised a plan of going to the Coliseum to arrange
the captured Christians' escape. This was most important to him.

Dr. G. This plan sounds a bit much for you to do
        alone.

Ivy.   It is. I went back to see Laramus, and he tried
        to talk me out of it.

Dr. G. And then?

Ivy.   Later, he agreed to help me.

So the plan was finalized. Laramus had as much hatred for
the Romans as Josephus, if not more; but he also valued his own
survival more, and Josephus's plan sounded suicidal. Laramus
was reluctant and Josephus shamed him for his reticence, but
neither man was thinking logically.

I progressed Josephus forward to the actual execution of his
plan.

Dr. G.   Where are you now?

Ivy.   I am in the Coliseum.

Dr. G.   Is it that simple to gain access to this sta-
dium?

Ivy.   When you are dressed as a soldier.

Dr. G.   Please continue.

Ivy.   There was a drunken Roman guard where the
Christians were imprisoned whom Laramus knocked unconscious.

Dr. G.   What happened next?

Ivy.   After we switched clothes, we dragged him out
into the arena.

Dr. G.   Since he was unconscious, didn't that raise
objections from the crowd?

Ivy.   He was coming to by the time the lions were
let loose.

Dr. G.   What did he do?

Ivy.   What do you think he did? He screamed and
ran but not fast or far enough. The lions
tore him apart. The crowd roared.

Dr. G.   What happened next?

Ivy.   I set the other Christians free while everyone's
attention was focused on the lions.

This must have been a strange day for Josephus. Here he
was, dressed as the symbol he most hated, a Roman soldier. While
he felt good about helping his fellow Christians to escape, what
about the guard who was needlessly killed? Josephus's newly
adopted "an-eye-for-an-eye" philosophy most certainly went
against his Christian beliefs.

But things moved too quickly for reflection now. Josephus saw Laramus, led by some Roman soldiers, coming toward him. Laramus would not even look at Josephus as the soldiers approached.

> Dr. G. What's going on, Josephus?
>
> Ivy. It's Laramus. He was captured, and he turned me in to save his own skin. That is why he can't even look at me in the eye. He is a traitor.
>
> Dr. G. What about the Christians you helped escape?
>
> Ivy. They got away, but it looks like I'm not so fortunate.

The guards had offered to spare Laramus if he led them to Josephus. Josephus was disarmed and thrown into the cell formerly occupied by the Christians.

> Dr. G. How do you feel at this time?
>
> Ivy. I don't care what happens to me. I just can't live in this society.
>
> Dr. G. What about Laramus?
>
> Ivy. That traitor. My lifelong friend turned me in to save his own miserable life. Well, it didn't work.
>
> Dr. G. What do you mean?
>
> Ivy. The guards lied to him; they put him in the same cell with me. He will die with me.
>
> Dr. G. Do you want to attack him now? After all, he is in the same cell with you.
>
> Ivy. No. It's all right now. Justice will be served. He will die, too.

Dr. G.   How does Laramus deal with this?

Ivy.   He actually threatened me. He told me he
would get even with me for dragging him
into my suicidal plan. No matter what it
would take, he will get me for this.

Shortly thereafter, they were both executed. Laramus died
first. Josephus almost seemed relieved to die.

From the superconscious level, I found out that Laramus
was John. While we might be tempted to identify this life as the
origin of the karmic vendetta that John had towards Ivy, karma,
as we have pointed out, simply doesn't work in a linear fashion.
Ultimately, all time is simultaneous, and we apparently function
in a space-time continuum. Again, I refer you to Wolf (1981) for
a more detailed explanation of time from the perspective of a
quantum physicist.

The most interesting dynamic of this regression is the fact
that Ivy and John weren't lovers. Their male-to-male friendship
was apparently a good one until, under pressure, John's true
personality emerged. He did not exhibit his full-blown violence,
but John is still John.

The Outline of History (409-410) provides some interesting
historical documentation for the social background described by
Ivy as Josephus:

> ...between 27 BC and AD 180.... was an age
> of spending rather than of creation, an age of
> architecture and trade in which the rich grew
> richer and the poor poorer and the soul and spirit
> of man decayed. Looked at superficially,...there
> was a considerable flourish of prosperity [charac-
> terized by] large and well-built cities, with tem-
> ples, theaters, amphitheaters, markets.... an
> abundant cultivation [based on] grudging work of

slaves.... There had been a softening of manners
and a general refinement since the days of Julius
Caesar.... Not only were the cities outwardly
more splendidly built, but within the homes of the
wealthy there had been great advances in the art
of decoration.... There was a considerable'
amount of what we may describe as "rich men's
culture" throughout the Empire.... and if the
prominent men of...the city lacked any profound
culture themselves, they could always turn to
some slave or other, whose learning had been
guaranteed of the highest quality by the slave
dealer, to supply the deficiency.

As usual, Ivy's relation of a past life correlates well with
historical details about which she had no information, and the
connection between Josephus and Laramus, though blighted by
betrayal in the end, reveals a gentler and more stable background
to the Ivy-John conflict. But it is time now to return to the darker
side of Ivy's karmic tableau to witness a further unfolding of the
web of violent passions that would ultimately be acted out in
Buffalo, New York, in 1927.

10: A MURDER AND SUICIDE

By now it had become routine for Ivy to enter my office, and within a short time, be living a past life. I never knew what to expect. Sometimes she began speaking with a deep voice; on other occasions, she barely whispered. These changes in voice inflection and name, accompanied by emotional expressions ranging from cold and distant to histrionic were now common-place. But the process was never boring. Ivy continued to press me to guide her through as many past lives as I could. It seemed almost as if she were looking for something beyond therapy.

Although every past-life regression is therapeutic when sessions are correctly conducted, it is not necessary to log dozens of experiences to attain therapeutic goals. The cleansing tech-niques described in Appendix A are far more efficient in attain-ing clinical effects. But, although most of her issues were resolved, Ivy seemed compelled by a driving curiosity concerning her past lives, even if it meant delaying the conclusion of her therapy, and I had no objection to "researching her karmic records" through other incarnations. Ivy seemed eager to experience the next past life as we began the session. And the regression that followed turned out to be an obvious prelude to her life as Grace Doze.

As had become clear from her other past-life regressions, Ivy attracted violent death experiences. It no longer shocked me when her past lives ended with her being publicly executed or murdered through some senseless act by her eternal perpetrator, John. The following case was to be no exception, but it would further illustrate the love triangle between Ivy, Dave and John. As is often the case in karmic relationships, the actors remain the same, but the roles of the characters change. Ivy seemed to be the perennial victim, and Dave usually the husband or boyfriend and an ally of Ivy. But in this past life, John becomes Ivy's husband, rather than the "other man"; his homicidal tendencies nonetheless rise to the surface.

> Dr. G.   Where do you find yourself?
>
> Ivy.   I'm a small child playing in my room.
>
> Dr. G.   Are you a little boy or girl?
>
> Ivy.   Oh, I'm a girl.
>
> Dr. G.   Tell me about your family.
>
> Ivy.   I have a mommy and a daddy and one big, mean brother.
>
> Dr. G.   Does your brother beat you?
>
> Ivy.   No, it's just that he is so much older than I am, and he won't play with me.
>
> Dr. G.   What does he do with his time?
>
> Ivy.   He works in the mill with Daddy.

Ivy was describing a life in a lower-class section of Philadelphia during the 1830's. Her father worked in a mill or factory, as did her eighteen-year-old brother. Ivy was nine years old, and her name in this life was Doris.

I next progressed Doris to a significant event in her life.

Dr. G. Doris, what is happening at this time?

Ivy. I don't feel well.

Dr. G. What is the matter?

Ivy. I have fever and chills, and I hurt all over.

Doris was a somewhat sickly child. She described a number of incidents of childhood illness that caused her to miss school often, and her parents literally feared for her life, especially during the cold winter months. As she grew older, Doris seemed to overcome this vulnerability to illness. She described a normal and happy teenage and young-adult life.

When I next met Doris, she was twenty-one and still living with her parents.

Dr. G. What are you up to these days, Doris?

Ivy. Oh, I'm still living with my parents. I do like Art, though.

Dr. G. What kind of art do you like?

Ivy. No, silly, I mean Arthur. I call him Art. He's my, you know, boyfriend.

Dr. G. What does Art do?

Ivy. He works in a factory.

Dr. G. With your father and brother?

Ivy. No, but he likes his work. I don't think my father and brother like what they do.

Dr. G. What is it that you like most about Art?

Ivy.   He's tall and, you know, handsome. Art says
        nice things to me.

Dr. G. How long have you been dating Art?

Ivy.   About six months.

Dr. G. Do you love him?

Ivy.   Yes, I think I do. He is the only boy I have
        ever known that knows how to make me
        feel like a real woman.

From other information Doris related to me, it appeared
that Art was something of a con artist. He knew how to please
Doris, but would periodically stand her up on a date or show up
late. He seemed to know the right thing to say to distract Doris
from the real issue and feed into her vulnerabilities. As Doris was
romantic, flowers or candy and some "sweet talking" would
always soften up her anger or frustration, and she would forgive
Art.

I next progressed Doris forward to an important event in
her relationship with Art.

Dr. G. Where are you now?

Ivy.   I'm over at Art's.

Dr. G. What is special about this particular day?

Ivy.   Art has asked me to marry him. I'm just so
        happy.

Dr. G. Do you accept?

Ivy.   Oh, yes. I can't wait for our wedding day!

Later on, a significant event occurred that proved to be
predictive of Art's personality.

Dr. G. Doris, you look upset. What has happened
        since we last spoke?

Ivy.   I don't know what to make of it.

Dr. G.   What are you referring to?

Ivy.   It's Art.

Dr. G.   What about Art?

Ivy.   He got into a fight with one of his buddies at work today and almost lost his job, and our wedding is less than a month away.

Dr. G.   What was the fight about?

Ivy.   Oh, it was just some stupid joke his friend made about getting married.

Dr. G.   Did this joke have anything to do with you personally?

Ivy.   No. It was just one of those stupid remarks that guys make about marriage in general. You know, like being in prison.

Dr. G.   That was it?

Ivy.   Yes. I talked to some of the guys who were there. Nothing was said about me.

Dr. G.   How serious was this fight?

Ivy.   It was very serious the way I heard it. Art came close to killing his pal, and over such a stupid thing like that. It just don't figure.

Dr. G.   Has he ever done anything like that before?

Ivy.   Well, he is very jealous. One time he was buying me an ice and some man I didn't know complimented me on my dress. Art took my ice and shoved it in the man's face. I was so embarrassed.

Dr. G.   Did you worry about this behavior?

      Ivy.   No. I just figured Art loves me and doesn't want any other man to show an interest in me. What's wrong with that?

Apparently Art had a violent temper along with a very jealous and insecure psyche. He never beat Doris, but he became quite possessive towards her, and it didn't help that Doris was very insecure in her own right. She needed a strong man to guide her in life. Art seemed superfically to fill this requirement. He was, at least, tall and physically powerful. Unfortunately, Doris could not or would not take note of his inner tension, insecurities and potentially violent nature.

I next progressed Doris to a time after her wedding to see how life was treating her.

      Dr. G. How are things going, Doris?

      Ivy.   Oh, just fine. Art and I are very happy.

      Dr. G. You don't sound happy.

      Ivy.   Well, maybe I'm just expecting too much from Art.

      Dr. G. What do you mean?

      Ivy.   Art likes to hunt on weekends.

      Dr. G. Go on.

      Ivy.   I don't mind that he hunts. My father gave him a shotgun for his birthday last year, and Art loves to go.

      Dr. G. I don't see the problem. Is Art spending too much time away from you?

      Ivy.   No, it's not that. It's just that when he comes home, I have to clean and prepare the game, and Art spends a lot of time cleaning and playing with that darn shotgun.

Dr. G. So, is that what is bothering you? Are you mad because of all this extra work?

Ivy. No, it's not that. It's just that lately he hasn't brought any game home.

Dr. G. It sounds like you should be grateful.

Ivy. No, you don't understand. He doesn't even use that gun when he goes away.

Dr. G. What do you mean?

Ivy. After he used to come home from these hunting trips, he would clean and oil his shotgun. He would take it apart, like a child playing with a toy.

Dr. G. So?

Ivy. But now he doesn't do that. I checked the gun before he left and after he got home. I know he never so much as fired one shot. That's just not like him. Maybe it's just me.

Art was having an affair with a tavern maid. He used his weekend hunting trips as an excuse to get away to see his lover. Doris just couldn't or wouldn't face up to facts, preferring to believe that she was reading too much into Art's actions, or that it was all her fault. She would never confront Art about this, even when his fellow workers' wives hinted to Doris about the affair. Doris just assumed it was a bad joke, or that his coworkers had it in for Art. After all, in her eyes, Art could do no wrong. Because she felt she wasn't good enough for him, she found it easy to overlook Art's faults. As we shall see, this proved to be a fatal mistake.

Next I progressed Doris forward to a significant event in her married life.

Dr. G. What is happening at this time?

Ivy.   Oh, I'm so happy! I just had a baby.

Dr. G.   Was it a boy or girl?

Ivy.   A girl. We named her Jean. She's so beautiful.

Dr. G.   How has Art been treating you lately?

Ivy.   Everything is okay.

Dr. G.   Has he shown his jealous side?

Ivy.   I don't know why you keep picking on him.
He is really a good man, and I'm lucky to
be his wife.

Doris was so emotionally invested in the relationship that she clung to anything that would distract her from dealing with the seedier realities of who Art was. I don't doubt for a moment that Doris loved her baby daughter Jean and I'm convinced that she was madly in love with Art. The problem was that she remained blind to Art's faults. She ignored his occasional temper, his jealousy, his adultery, and even his drunkenness.

It appears that Art was not as happy with his job at the factory as he led Doris to believe. Perhaps this was just one of his "lines" to her. The reality was that he was bored and depressed. His affairs and frequent tavern visits were his dysfunctional way of dealing with life's stresses. Since he had never turned his violence on Doris, she did not feel threatened.

One interesting development at this time had to do with her baby daughter. Jean became ill often, which reminded Doris of her own childhood. She didn't want her baby to go through what she had. Doris and Art were far from affluent. They were a young, struggling couple with a sickly daughter. Seeing a physician regularly was simply out of the question. They could not afford it.

One of Doris's friends told her of a doctor who charged lower fees to people who couldn't afford medical care. Doris began taking Jean to Dr. Barry. Barry was the young physician's first name, but everyone simply referred to him as Dr. Barry.

> Dr. G. How is Jean doing?
>
> Ivy.   Oh, she is okay now. Dr. Barry is a saint.
>
> Dr. G. What exactly is wrong with Jean?
>
> Ivy.   I don't know. She just gets sick a lot, especially in the winter. I used to do that.

Apparently Jean inherited Doris's weak immune system. Doris felt confident that Jean would outgrow this problem, just as she had done.

> Dr. G. Tell me more about Dr. Barry.
>
> Ivy.   Well, he is a nice man, and Jean really likes him.
>
> Dr. G. How do you feel about him?
>
> Ivy.   I like him, too. He talks to me about lots of things. I mean, he is a doctor yet he doesn't scare me.

Doris was easily intimidated by any authority figure. This explained her tendency to overlook faults in Art, who, after all, was an authority figure to her.

Doris also mentioned sharing many common interests with Dr. Barry. They both liked poetry and plants. Dr. Barry had a talent for growing things. Once in a while, he would give Doris one of his "creations" when she brought Jean to his office. They became friends in this way. But Doris's contact with Dr. Barry was limited to her trips to the office with Jean.

> Dr. G. How does Art feel about Jean's medical problems?

Ivy.   Well, um, he isn't very patient with her. You know how men are. He sometimes yells at her and demands that she get better.

Dr. G.   Doesn't that bother you?

Ivy.   Not really. I realize how tough it is for him. After all, Art is a strong man. I mean, I have never seen him sick. Even as a boy, he was always fit.

Dr. G.   Whereas you can identify with Jean.

Ivy.   That's right. I know what it is like to be sickly. After all, you can't blame Art for not understanding, can you?

Of course not. How could one possibly blame this insecure, possessive, obsessively jealous, yet insensitive, adulterous, and depressed man? Doris, at any rate, couldn't.

Doris and Dr. Barry developed a platonic friendship. Barry was a highly moral man who was very dedicated to his work and very sensitive to the needs of his patients. Dr. Barry was single, in his late twenties, and lived alone in a small flat in downtown Philadelphia. He seemed to truly care for Doris, without being interested in her sexually.

Doris viewed their friendship as a welcome novelty in her dreary life. She had few friends, and her family didn't seem to have much respect for her. Doris's insecurity projected rather strongly to most of the people with whom she interacted. Her motivation in fostering a friendship with Dr. Barry was based on emotional needs, not on a desire for an affair. When I asked Ivy about Dr. Barry, she would always speak fondly of him. Her voice would be soft, and she would relax more in the recliner in my office.

Dr. G.   Can you tell me more about your relationship with Dr. Barry?

Ivy.   What would you like to know?

Dr. G. Do you ever see him outside of his office?

Ivy.   Yes, but it's not what you think.

Dr. G. How did this come about?

Ivy.   Well, one night Jean had a real emergency. I
        mean, she was gasping for breath and had
        a high fever. I sent for Dr. Barry, and he
        came over to our flat.

Dr. G. What happened next?

Ivy.   Dr. Barry was wonderful. He treated Jean and
        stayed with her until the fever broke.

Dr. G. Was your husband home at the time?

Ivy.   Yes, Art was there.

Dr. G. You don't sound very happy about that.

Ivy.   Well, it was really embarrassing. I mean, Art
        acted so dumb. He resented Dr. Barry's
        presence right from the beginning. Right
        away he didn't like him. I know for a fact
        that Art had never met Dr. Barry before.

It's easy for you, the reader, and me to understand the
significance of this karmic carryover. Art had a natural disdain
for Dr. Barry. Art's subconscious mind recognized Dave from
numerous other past-life involvements, like a dog's recognizing
someone by scent, even though he is wearing a disguise and looks
totally different. This instant negative chemistry was also perceived by Dr. Barry. The good doctor didn't know where it came
from, because he knew he had never met Art before, at least not
in this lifetime. As far as Doris knew, neither Art nor Dr. Barry
experienced any form of spontaneous flashbacks, dreams or
other psychic phenomena. It was just a bad feeling.

During this house call, Art did everything he could to make Dr. Barry feel unwelcome. Doris had to constantly apologize for his actions. When Dr. Barry had completed his treatment of Jean, Art didn't even show common courtesy by thanking him. He merely went to bed and told Dr. Barry to show himself out. Dr. Barry, however, did not feel animosity toward Art. He merely felt uncomfortable in his presence. It is no wonder; in light of the number of times Art's soul had murdered Dr. Barry's essence, I'm surprised he didn't manifest a full-blown panic attack the moment he laid eyes on Art.

In a few months, Dr. Barry invited Doris to a poetry reading. She readily accepted and told Art where she was going. He became angry and jealous but, surprisingly, did not forbid her to go.

Dr. G.   Tell me about your date with Dr. Barry.

Ivy.   It's not a date in that sense, you know. Really, can't a lady spend some time in the company of a gentleman without its being seen as "dirty"?

Dr. G.   How did you like the poetry reading?

Ivy.   Oh, it was heaven! I mean, there were some really sensitive and intelligent people there. When they read their poetry, they became so emotional.

Dr. G.   What did you do afterwards?

Ivy.   Well, we went to get some coffee and talked.

Dr. G.   Are you developing romantic feelings towards Dr. Barry?

Ivy.   I really don't think of him that way. I know as a man you may find that hard to believe, but it's the truth.

Dr. G. I believe you, Doris. What about Dr. Barry?
Do you sense that he is developing those
feelings about you?

Ivy. Again, I would have to say no. I can't read his
mind, but a woman sort of knows these
things. He is very kind and considerate but
always a gentleman. If I can't see him or
meet him some place, he doesn't act the
same as Art would, or any boy I dated before I was married. He doesn't act in a jealous way or become dejected or sad.

Dr. G. Do you see him often alone?

Ivy. No, not really. Sometimes we go shopping for
plants. Other times, we just have coffee or
go for a walk.

Dr. G. What do you two talk about?

Ivy. Oh, lots of things. He always asks about Jean,
of course. We talk about poetry, plants,
and nature. He tells me about his family.

Dr. G. Does he ever mention a girlfriend?

Ivy. No, he never does. He is a shy man, and I
really think that most women scare him.
You know, it's like he is very inexperienced.

Dr. G. Does that bother you?

Ivy. No, of course not. I think it's kind of sweet. It
makes me feel special knowing that he
feels secure around me. I also feel hon-
ored to be in his company.

Doris truly enjoyed the time she spent with Dr. Barry. She
convinced me that she was not sexually attracted to him, and that

his interest in her also had a platonic agenda. Dr. Barry's standing in the community as a physician, his sensitivity and positive demeanor, along with many common interests formed the basis of this friendship.

Art, however, could not accept so innocent an explanation. He constantly interrogated Doris about her relationship with Dr. Barry. Still, he would not forbid her to see him, as evidenced by the following exchange:

Dr. G. Does your friendship with Dr. Barry cause any problems with your husband?

Ivy. Well, yes, it does.

Dr. G. How so?

Ivy. Art argues with me more now. At first, I thought it was his job. Now, I realize that he misinterprets my relationship with Dr. Barry.

Dr. G. What makes you conclude that?

Ivy. He mentions Dr. Barry's name a lot, and when he does, he pounds his fist on the kitchen table. Also, he looks at me funny when he knows I am going out to meet him.

Dr. G. Does he ever forbid you to see Dr. Barry?

Ivy. No. That's just it. It's almost as if he wants to have something to argue about. He never forbids me to see Dr. Barry. I, of course, never bring up that topic.

Dr. G. Does he ever strike you?

Ivy. No, he hasn't yet, but I am getting a little worried.

Dr. G. Why is that?

Ivy.   In the last few weeks he has come close to hitting me.

Dr. G. Have you told your family or friends your concerns?

Ivy.   No…no, I haven't. I'll work it out.

That was Doris's typically passive response to this potentially explosive situation. From an observer's perspective, however, there was reason to be very concerned about the probable outcome. Art came from a violent family. His father was an alcoholic who beat Art regularly during his formative years. Art never could strike back at his father, even when, at sixteen, he was taller and stronger. He had learned to repress his feelings, especially anger. Art released this anger by getting into street fights or barroom brawls.

It is this type of repression that concerns the therapist the most. Art was an explosion waiting to happen. He sublimated anger and violent tendencies toward Doris (and Jean, I later discovered) by having affairs, and in hunting. When he stopped hunting, this left only his mistress, whom Art gave up after nearly getting himself shot by the jealous husband one night about a year later. He kept repressing his anger during the next three years until finally an incident occurred that replicated Ivy's and John's karmic patterns.

Jean was five years old and became very ill late one afternoon with the symptoms of pneumonia, and Doris did not want to wait until she could get word to Dr. Barry to make a house call. Dr. Barry had instructed her to bring Jean in anytime such symptoms developed; Jean could die if not attended.

Doris left a note for Art, who was due home from work soon, stating that she had gone to Dr. Barry's for emergency treatment for Jean. She was even considerate enough to prepare Art's dinner before leaving, but, as we shall see, this was not enough to placate Art, who arrived home in his usual bad mood, read the note, and went into a rage. He tore up the note, broke a chair in the kitchen and threw the dinner Doris had prepared for him on the floor. Nothing would calm him down now.

Common sense and logic were never Art's strong points. He had frequently fantasized that Doris lied to him about Dr. Barry and herself. When he noticed Doris had packed some extra clothes and taken Jean he was convinced she had left him. Art became obsessed with the idea that Doris and Dr. Barry must be making love and laughing at him behind his back. This was the last straw. He had to do something right now, and the only thing he could think of was killing Doris and Dr. Barry.

Since he had been to Dr. Barry's a few times, he knew where it was. He grabbed his shotgun and rushed out. Arriving at Dr. Barry's flat, Art kicked in the front door. Two other patients in the waiting room on this rather cold and dreary winter evening immediately ran out of the building, absolutely frightened, leaving just Doris and Jean there.

Dr. G. What happened next?

Ivy. I...I don't really know except that it all seems to have happened in slow motion. First, I jumped up and screamed at Art.

Dr. G. What did he do?

Ivy. He just started cussing at me and accusing me of leaving him for Dr. Barry.

Dr. G. Where was Dr. Barry at this time?

Ivy. He was in his laboratory getting some medicine ready.

Dr. G. Why was Jean in the waiting room with you now?

Ivy. Oh, he just finished with a patient and I...I mean Jean was next.

Dr. G.   Then what happened?

Ivy.   Like I said, it was a blur. (Ivy was very emotional.) Art picked up his shotgun and shot Jean in the head. Oh, my God! Then, before I could do anything, he shot me, too.

I guided Doris (Ivy) into the superconscious mind level so she could overview the entire situation.

Dr. G.   From this perspective, now that you are in spirit, please tell me what happened next.

Ivy.   Art killed Jean and me. Dr. Barry came running out to the waiting room as soon as he heard the shots.

Dr. G.   Go on.

Ivy.   Art was reloading the shotgun. Dr. Barry began struggling with him, but before he could get the gun away, Art turned it on himself and pulled the trigger.

The reception room was a horror. There was blood everywhere. The police came eventually and helped clean up the place, but Dr. Barry remained in a state of shock and was never the same after this incident.

In this life, Dave, as Dr. Barry, was once again his humane and nurturing self, and John, as Art, revealed himself to be a deranged and dangerous man who finally exploded more violently than ever, leaving a bloody spectacle of bodies on the stage where Ivy's karmic ballet had been danced yet again. Ivy was again John's victim, and, in keeping with the pattern which had emerged, died swiftly and impersonally through his violent instrumentation. But as we were soon to see, Ivy had died yet another and more brutal death at John's hands, a modern culmination of the destructive karmic embrace with which, through time and times, he had repeatedly sought to destroy her.

The period in which the events in Philadelphia occurred is similar enough to the present that Ivy's relation was not distinguished by many idiosyncrasies that could be checked against the cultural history of the time, though certainly nothing in her description was inconsistent with life in that era. It was in Ivy's one remaining past life, however, that we were to find detailed material for documentation beyond the wildest expectations of anyone who has ever explored this area of past-life regression.

11: THE DEATH OF GRACE

My purpose in conducting all past-life regressions is for therapeutic reasons, not historic research. By the time I regressed Ivy to her past life as Grace Doze, she had worked out her obsession with John and no longer needed him in her life. Ivy was involved with Dave in a healthy, loving relationship. From my perspective as a therapist, Ivy's treatment was complete. But Ivy was not yet content. It seemed there was something else she needed to unearth from her karmic past. She insisted that I regress her one more time.

As it happened, a final clinical detail Ivy never had told me about prior to this forty-sixth past-life regression was resolved in its course. That issue dealt with her fear of choking. It seems that Ivy could not wear turtleneck sweaters and became very upset— almost a panic disorder—whenever anyone, even Dave, would touch her neck, even playfully. I included this issue in my instructions prior to her regression.

Ivy and I had agreed this was to be her last regression. Neither of us knew this particular past-life exploration would require a few sessions, as it led us into the lurid tangle of the short, tragic life of Grace Doze.

Dr. G. Where do you find yourself at this time?

Ivy.   I'm in my mother's home, arguing with my husband.

Dr. G. What is your name?

Ivy.   Grace.

Dr. G.   What year is it?

Ivy.   1925.

Dr. G. What is this argument about?

Ivy.   Chester is asking me about my activities.

Dr. G   What activities are those?

Ivy.   My idiot husband is accusing me of seeing other men.

Dr. G. Is he correct?

Ivy.   Of course he is right. You don't for the moment think that he could possibly keep me happy?

Dr. G. Do you have any children?

Ivy.   Yes, we have a son named Cliff.

Dr. G. Where is he at this time while you are having this fight?

Ivy.   Cliff is out with my mother. I don't want him to witness these fights if I can help it.

Ivy manifested a very different personality profile in this past life. She was a cold and calculating woman named Grace who had little respect and much dislike for her husband Chester.

Dr. G.   Grace, where do you live?

Ivy.   Buffalo.

Dr. G.   What kind of work does Chester do?

Ivy.   The idiot works for General Electric.

Dr. G.   Why did you marry him?

Ivy.   I don't know. If I had to do it again, I would still be single. At least I can act like I'm single.

Dr. G.   You mean by having affairs?

Ivy.   Yeah. Why not? I'm an attractive, thirty-year-old woman in my prime. Why shouldn't I go out and enjoy myself?

Dr. G.   Tell me more about your argument with Chester.

Ivy.   What do you want to know?

Dr. G.   Is this just a verbal fight?

Ivy.   This is, yeah. But many times he hits me, and I hit him back.

Dr. G.   Do you feel physically threatened?

Ivy.   I can handle myself. He may be bigger than me, but I get my two cents in, and I'm not letting any man run my life, least of all that idiot. I don't care if my mother sees us going at it. I will not listen to Chester.

I then questioned Grace further about her husband Chester.

Dr. G. Tell me more about your husband.

Ivy. You mean Chester, the boring, Doze.

Dr. G. Yes.

Ivy. Well, there's not much to tell. He was in the Army a while back. He works for General Electric and is usually covered with dirt when he comes home.

Dr. G. Please continue.

Ivy. Chester is very quiet when we are not fighting. He just sits in his easy chair and stares out the window. His name is just like his personality, Doze. If he could, he would probably sleep all day.

Grace definitely had a caustic sense of humor. Her quips, however, had revealed her last name, Doze. Normally I am not interested in a patient's last name in a previous life. In this case, however, it turned out to be significant in documenting Ivy's prior life.

Dr. G. Grace, you say Chester is quiet and dull. How would you describe yourself?

Ivy. I like excitement. I must be active. Seeing other men is just part of having fun and good times.

Grace went on to describe many incidents with other men. She was in the habit of going to speakeasies with her girlfriends or with one of her many men. This was the mid-1920's. Prohibition was the law of the land, so it was not all that easy to go out on the town and celebrate with alcohol. You could, of course, if you knew the right people and were informed about where to go. Grace was well informed.

The following year, 1926, Grace moved to what she described as the Main Street apartment with Chester and Cliff. This place was not far from her mother's home.

Dr. G.　Is it difficult to get away for a rendezvous?

Ivy.　No, not really. My mother's house is over on Chester Street, and she likes taking care of my son Cliff. He spends a lot of time with his grandmother.

Dr. G.　Excuse me, Grace, but didn't you say that your husband's name is Chester?

Ivy.　Yeah, so what?

Dr. G.　You described your mother's house as being on Chester Street.

Ivy.　She does live on Chester Street. It's just a coincidence.

In parapsychology there are no coincidences. I questioned her further about her activities.

Dr. G.　How do you get around town so easily?

Ivy.　That's part of the fun. I thumb rides from guys in cars. It's a great way to meet a good-looking man.

Dr. G.　Isn't it somewhat dangerous?

Ivy.　You sound like my husband. I suppose you sit in a chair all day and stare out the window.

Dr. G.　You didn't answer my question.

Ivy.　I guess it could be dangerous. Sometimes I run into a creep. So what? After all, I married a jerk.

Dr. G.　Do you hitchhike alone?

| Ivy. | Sometimes. Other times, me and my girl-friends thumb rides together. Some guys like it when they have two fun-loving women, if you know what I mean. My best friend Mary could tell you some pretty interesting stories. |

Grace was a real Roaring Twenties party girl. She was responsible enough to not abandon her son Cliff, but beyond that her lifestyle was hedonistic.

This was quite a change from Ivy's other lives, though it should be pointed out that the fact that this was her last lifetime did not mean that this life was more significant than previous ones. The importance of any life is in how one grows and learns from the experience and thus raises the vibrational frequency of his or her subconscious mind.

| Dr. G. | Tell me more about these affairs. Are some of these men married? |

| Ivy. | Oh, yes. They make some of the best lovers. I do things that their wives won't, and they can be more relaxed with me. |

| Dr. G. | Isn't it hard to find a place for these dates? |

| Ivy. | No. I just rent a room somewhere and use it for as long as I like. |

| Dr. G. | How do you find the time, and where do you get the money to rent these rooms? Do you work? |

| Ivy. | No. I'm just a housewife. The guys I hang out with are very generous, and they don't mind giving me some extra spending money. |

| Dr. G. | Do you use the same place all the time? |

Ivy.   No, I don't want to worry about my snoopy
husband finding me, or the wife of one of
my guys.

Dr. G.   But you said that Chester knows about
these other men.

Ivy.   He knows I see other men. He doesn't know
who, or where I go, and I have no intention of making it easy for him to find that
out. I always register under a different
name. Smart, huh?

Dr. G.   It doesn't sound like your marriage is a particularly happy one.

Ivy.   My marriage is like my maiden name, Loveless.

Grace's sarcastic sense of humor was working for me again.
This time she had given me her maiden name, which also proved
significant in documenting this life.

Dr. G.   It sounds like you flaunt your affairs in your
husband's face.

Ivy.   I guess I do. Do you want to know what I do
under his nose?

Dr. G.   Yes, please continue.

Ivy.   I have my dates meet me at the corner by the
Main Street apartment. Isn't that funny? I
can see them coming from the window.
Chester is so stupid he doesn't even notice
them.

Grace liked to refer to the various places she stayed by the
streets they were located on, which also provided material for
documentation.

Dr. G.   Tell me about your mother.

Ivy.   What would you like to know?

Dr. G. How does she feel about Chester?

Ivy.   I can never figure her out. She actually likes that idiot and tries to make peace between us. My mother is very conservative, just the opposite of me. I don't listen to her, and sometimes I don't even tell her what I'm up to when I go out.

Dr. G. Doesn't Chester know that she takes care of Cliff when you are out for the evening?

Ivy.   Yeah, of course he does. He's stupid but not that dumb. Mom doesn't like it when he comes around looking for me. She just lies to him, and he goes away.

Dr. G. So Chester looks for you when you are on a date?

Ivy.   Oh, yeah. He's a real snoop. He walks all over town looking for me. I hear about it from some of the hotel clerks. He's always asking around about me. Fortunately, he is a lousy detective.

By this time, I was getting a pretty good picture of Ivy's life as Grace Doze. Grace liked to keep men guessing, especially Chester. She teased the men she picked up, and this sometimes led to violence. This was illustrated by an incident in the year 1926.

Dr. G. Where are you now, Grace?

Ivy.   I'm in a car outside the Tourist Hotel.

Dr. G. Are you alone?

Ivy. Of course I'm not alone. The guy who owns this buggy picked me up a while ago when I was thumbing for a ride.

Dr. G. Go on.

Ivy. Well, we went out for dinner and some drinks, and I played with him.

Dr. G. What do you mean? Is this one of your boy-friends?

Ivy. No. I just met him. I had nothing else better to do and no money, so I tricked him into tak-ing me out.

Dr. G. What do you mean, tricked him?

Ivy. I told him I would show him a good time if he took me out.

Dr. G. Go on.

Ivy. Well, I don't really like him, and I have no in-tention of sleeping with him. I told him to take me to this hotel.

Dr. G. What are you going to do now?

Ivy. When he goes in to get a room, I'm going to cut out on him.

Her suitor did go to obtain a room for them, and Ivy jumped out of the car. The problem was that he saw her leave the car and ran after her.

Dr. G. What happened?

Ivy. That gorilla hit me. He caught me and called me all sorts of names and started slapping me.

Dr. G. Are you hurt bad?

> Ivy.   No. I'm okay. You can't win them all.

This incident meant little to Grace. She wasn't in the habit of considering other people's feelings when she acted. Grace did virtually whatever she wanted, whenever she wanted, and with whomever happened to be around.

Her relationship with Chester was very volatile. She seemed to pick fights just to annoy him. He, on the other hand, was not a happy man and was easily dragged into Grace's cat-and-mouse games.

> Dr. G.   Do you see your girlfriends much?
>
> Ivy.   Oh, yes. We go swimming at the high school, and shopping, of course.
>
> Dr. G.   And do you go out with them to pick up men?
>
> Ivy.   Sure. We know how to have a good time. Mary and I really know how to have fun.
>
> Dr. G.   How old is Cliff?
>
> Ivy.   He is two.
>
> Dr. G.   Having him around must slow you down.

I was trying to get a reaction from Grace concerning her family responsibilities. When I made this statement, Ivy just sat motionless in my recliner and started crying. This was the first time Grace exhibited emotions.

> Dr. G.   What is it, Grace? What is making you so sad?
>
> Ivy.   Cliff is very important to me. He's more than just my son.
>
> Dr. G.   What do you mean?

> Ivy.   I was married before, and I had a boy but he
>   died. I lost another child after that, too.

Ivy started crying again. This was a very emotional point for
her. At least in this area Grace showed some feeling for someone
other than herself.

I progressed Grace forward again.

> Dr. G. What has happened since I last spoke to
>   you?

> Ivy.   I'm having a fight with Chester.

> Dr. G. Are you at home now?

> Ivy.   Yes, if you call it that.

> Dr. G. What's going on?

> Ivy.   Chester came over to my mother's house and
>   demanded I bring Cliff and return home.

> Dr. G. What did you do?

> Ivy.   At first, I just told him to leave me alone, but
>   then he mentioned Guido.

> Dr. G. Who is Guido?

> Ivy.   Chester doesn't know Guido, but he told me
>   he saw me with a tall, muscular Italian
>   man wearing a silk suit last night.

> Dr. G. Did he mention Guido's name?

> Ivy.   No, but the description is accurate enough.
>   Anyway, I went out with Guido last night,
>   and I knew my idiot husband was going to
>   start a fight. I don't want that at my
>   mother's. She's heard enough of our
>   fights. She has enough problems of her
>   own.

Dr. G. Then what happened?

Ivy. We went home and Chester started yelling at me. He called me a whore and slapped me across the face.

Dr. G. What did you do?

Ivy. I threw a vase at him, and it broke against the wall. I then punched him in the stomach, and we started going at it.

Dr. G. What about Cliff?

Ivy. He was crying with all the noise that we made, but I couldn't deal with him at that moment.

Dr. G. Go on.

Ivy. Well, he hit me a few more times, and I told him that Guido was ten times the man he could ever be.

Dr. G. What did Chester do then?

Ivy. He stopped fighting. He just sat down in his favorite chair and started crying. How can I respect a man like that? He just started crying like a baby.

Dr. G. What did you do then?

Ivy. I left and went over to my girlfriend's apartment for some peace and quiet and to catch up on some sleep.

That was how Grace typically handled tense situations. She simply left and became involved in something else. Chester, a boyfriend, her mother or anyone else—Grace had the ability to just tune them out and go on to something else. When she went over to her girlfriend's apartment, she didn't even mention the incident. "You can't win them all."

Grace looked for any possible excuse to get out of her apartment and away from Chester.

> Dr. G. Grace, have you ever thought of divorcing Chester?
>
> Ivy. Every day. One of these days I'm going to leave that apartment with Cliff and never return. I mean that; I really do.

As we shall see later, this was a most prophetic remark.

I progressed Grace forward to an incident she would find meaningful.

> Dr. G. Grace, where are you at this time?
>
> Ivy. I'm with Barney.
>
> Dr. G. Is he one of your boyfriends?
>
> Ivy. I just met him. He's fun. He likes to do crazy things, and he has a car.
>
> Dr. G. How did you meet Barney?
>
> Ivy. I was thumbing a ride. I told you, it's a great way to meet men.
>
> Dr. G. Is Barney living in Buffalo?
>
> Ivy. No. He is from Chicago and here in town on business.
>
> Dr. G. What kind of work does he do?
>
> Ivy. I don't know and I don't care. Talking about jobs is boring. I just want to have fun today.
>
> Dr. G. Where are you going?

Ivy.   We're going to Niagara Falls. I love watching the water.

I progressed Grace forward to an event that would be significant.

Dr. G.   What is happening now?

Ivy.   (Giggling) It's so much fun. I can't believe the look on his face.

Dr. G.   What is it?

Ivy.   Me and Barney were fooling around by the falls, and we got close to the edge. One of these guys that works there started yelling at us and chased us out. What a jerk!

Grace just didn't seem to respect any form of structure. These transient dates became the rule rather than the exception in her life.

Dr. G.   Where are you now, Grace?

Ivy.   I'm at the Main Street apartment fighting with my idiot husband.

Dr. G.   Is he being physically abusive to you?

Ivy.   No. He objects to my clothes.

Dr. G.   What about your clothes?

Ivy.   He says I look like a tramp when I go out.

Dr. G.   Is he referring to anything in particular?

Ivy.   Yes, it's my skirt. He says it's too short; they make me look cheap. He also doesn't like me wearing red. But I know it looks great on me.

I usually pay little attention to such details when I am conducting a past-life regression, but, as we shall see, this conversation would prove very significant in establishing the validity of Ivy's past life as Grace Doze.

> **Dr. G.** What did you do after Chester called you cheap?
>
> **Ivy.** I cursed him and grabbed my purse and ran down the steps and went out the door to visit my mother.

Again, Grace abandoned a tense situation and took off. Her mother was so used to hearing these stories that she thought nothing of them. Grace then rented a room and stayed away from her home for two days. After that, she returned to the Main Street apartment, and the cycle began all over again.

I next progressed Grace forward again.

> **Dr. G.** What year is this?
>
> **Ivy.** 1927.
>
> **Dr. G.** How are things with you?
>
> **Ivy.** All my idiot husband seems to care about is baseball.
>
> **Dr. G.** Is there any special man in your life at this time?
>
> **Ivy.** Yes. I'm seeing Jake now.
>
> **Dr. G.** Tell me about Jake.
>
> **Ivy.** He is new to town. Jake is tall and very strong. I don't know much about his background except that he is a bootlegger, and he has plenty of cash to spend.
>
> **Dr. G.** Where did you meet him?

Ivy.   I was at a speakeasy one night, alone and bored, and he walked up to me and introduced himself.

Dr. G.   Have you know him long?

Ivy.   No, just a week.

This was quite typical of Grace. The way she described Jake and their activities together did not make this relationship particularly unusual. It was spring of 1927.

Jake and Grace saw quite a bit of each other during the next few weeks. I then moved her forward to a significant event.

Dr. G.   Where are you now, Grace?

Ivy.   I'm fighting with Chester.

Dr. G.   Another war of words?

Ivy.   No. He hit me and I'm punching him. I hate him. When I told him I was leaving for good, he called me a bitch and slapped me.

Dr. G.   What did you do?

Ivy.   I really thought he was going to hurt me, so I grabbed a pair of scissors and told him to leave me alone.

Dr. G.   Then what happened?

Ivy.   He came at me and I stabbed him in the arm with the scissors. Then I ran out of the apartment. I was so scared I almost fell down the stairs.

Dr. G.   Where was your son Cliff at this time?

Ivy.   I brought him to my mother's earlier and told her I would join them later for supper.

This act of violence didn't seem to mean much to Grace. She expressed no concern about Chester's wound and stayed away from her apartment for a few days. I next progressed her forward by about two weeks.

Dr. G. What has happened since I last spoke to you?

Ivy. I really like Jake.

Dr. G. How does he feel about you?

Ivy. He must care for me. He tells me he didn't like Buffalo when he first came here, and I know he was supposed to leave in May. But now he says he is sure he will stay.

Dr. G. Please continue.

Ivy. He likes everything I do. Even when I go swimming every Tuesday at the high school, he takes me there and picks me up. He calls me his little mermaid.

Dr. G. Other than this being your current relationship, how does this affair differ from others that you have had?

Ivy. I'm leaving Chester.

This was a bombshell. Grace was quite serious about divorcing Chester. In the past she would have affairs and threaten to leave her husband, but now she was actually doing something about it.

Dr. G. Are you seeing other men at this time in addition to Jake?

Ivy. Yes, I do go out with other guys. That's only natural. But I like Jake the best.

Dr. G. Have you told Jake your plans?

> Ivy.   Yes, of course I have. You know, it's really
>   strange. Ever since I met him, I've been un-
>   able to keep him out of my mind.
>
> Dr. G.   What is it about Jake that makes him so
>   unique?
>
> Ivy.   I don't know. He is not the handsomest man I
>   know. It's just some crazy kind of thing
>   that I can't explain. I must be with him.

Grace couldn't explain this attraction, but I didn't have
trouble understanding the origin of the chemistry.

> Dr. G.   Have you told anyone else about your plans
>   to leave Chester?
>
> Ivy.   My mother and Mary know about it.
>
> Dr. G.   Have you confronted Chester yet?
>
> Ivy.   No, I don't want to fight all weekend. I'll wait
>   'til he goes back to work Monday.

They say the husband is always the last to know. Grace and
Chester didn't stress communication in their relationship. Grace
was about to make a major move in her life, and she still hadn't
told her husband.

> Dr. G.   Do you have a plan as to where you will go?
>
> Ivy.   Yes. I'm going to my mother's house for din-
>   ner on the 16th. After I tell Chester, I'm
>   not going to want to stick around. And
>   then Jake and I will go out for some fun.
>   I'll spend the night in the Tourist Hotel. I
>   have some clothes packed.
>
> Dr. G.   Go on.
>
> Ivy.   Tuesday Jake's going to drive me to the high
>   school to go swimming as usual. Then he

> will pick me up and take me back to the
> Tourist Hotel.

Dr. G. What about Cliff?

Ivy.   I'll get him on Wednesday and bring him back
        to the hotel.

Dr. G. Is Jake going to live with you?

Ivy.   Yes. He has a few things to do first, so it may
        take him a week or so before he finally
        moves in with us. He wants me to find a
        more permanent place in town for us.

Dr. G. By us you mean Cliff and you?

Ivy.   Of course.

Dr. G. How does Jake get along with Cliff?

Ivy.   Jake isn't used to children. I'm sure he will
        grow on him.

Dr. G. Has Jake spent much time with Cliff?

Ivy.   To tell you the truth, he hasn't even met him
        yet.

Grace was not a global planner. She had no idea as to
whether Jake and Cliff would get along. Although Jake new about
Cliff, he didn't know Grace had planned to take him with her to
the Tourist Hotel. The significance of this dysfunctional communication will be apparent soon.

Dr. G. Have any of your girlfriends met Jake yet?

Ivy.   Yeah, just Mary. I can always trust her to keep
        her mouth shut. After we get settled, we
        plan to throw a housewarming party.

Dr. G. Do your friends know what Jake does for a
        living?

> Ivy.   Yeah, but who cares?

What is unusual about this is that Grace habitually discussed her men with all her girlfriends. Their opinion of these suitors was very important to her. In this case, she solicited no such feedback, except from Mary. From a karmic perspective, this was quite significant, and I decided to follow up on this change in Grace's pattern.

> Dr. G.   Tell me a little more about your relation-ship with Jake. Are there any problems?
>
> Ivy.   I wouldn't think so. We get along real good, and we are both hot-blooded.
>
> Dr. G.   Are you both hot-tempered?
>
> Ivy.   We don't fight, if that's what you mean. I mean, me and Chester, we fight. We beat on each other. But me and Jake, we're good for each other.
>
> Dr. G.   Does Jake do anything to upset you?
>
> Ivy.   Not really. He is a little jealous of me, but that only shows how much he loves me.

Grace was living under a false impression that jealousy equates with love. In fact, jealousy is only a sign of insecurity, and it is because of this underlying neurosis that it can easily lead to violence.

> Dr. G.   Have you ever seen Jake angry?
>
> Ivy.   Not at me, but there was a time about a week ago when I was waiting for him to pick me up for a date.
>
> Dr. G.   Please continue.
>
> Ivy.   I was standing by this intersection when I saw a car just like Jake's. It was dark, and when

> the car slowed down, I went up to it and re-
> alized it wasn't Jake.

Dr. G. What did you do?

Ivy. The driver was nice and tried to pick me up. If
I wasn't expecting Jake, I probably would
have gone with him. He was real nifty looking, and he thought I was thumbing for a
ride.

Dr. G. What did Jake do?

Ivy. Oh, I almost forgot. Jake pulled up behind
this man and grabbed him by his collar
and punched him right in the nose.

Dr. G. What happened then?

Ivy. I was taken by surprise. I mean, it was almost
funny.

Dr. G What did Jake say to you?

Ivy. He told me to get in and said that if he ever
saw me with another man, he would kill
both of us.

Dr. G. Did that frighten you?

Ivy. No. I thought it showed how much he cared
for me. Anyway, men talk. I don't think he
was serious.

Grace may not have seen a reason for concern, but she most
certainly had one. I progressed her forward to Saturday, which
was May 14, 1927.

Dr. G. Grace, what have you been up to?

Ivy. I had my hair cut and went shopping for this
little black suitcase and I saw this blue out-
fit with a short, sexy skirt, and these beauti-

ful black shoes with red heels. Everything
Chester hates and Jake loves is in this
getup.

Next I progressed Grace forward to Monday, May 16.

Dr. G.   Did you confront Chester yet?

Ivy.   Yes, I told the fool, and we got into a fight.
Then do you know what he did? He
started to cry and begged me not to leave
him. Can you believe that loser?

Grace went right over to her mother's house and told her
mother the details of her plan. Grace knew that Chester would
probably come by in the next couple of days, so she told her
mother to keep Cliff in her house and not to tell Chester where
she was.

Dr. G.   What is going on now?

Ivy.   I told my mother that I'm going to Toronto to
see my friend Cathy.

Dr. G.   How will your mother answer Chester's
questions about your whereabouts?

Ivy.   I told her to go ahead and tell him that I'm going to Toronto for a few days. Even my
mother doesn't know that this story is a
lie, and that I will really be spending the
time with Jake.

Grace followed her plan. She packed some clothes and went
out with Jake. They spent the night together at the Tourist Hotel.
I progressed Grace forward to Tuesday, May 17.

Dr. G.   How are things going?

Ivy.   Okay, except for my idiot husband. I have
been running around all day to get moved,

and Chester decides to come by my
mother's house now.

Dr. G. What does he say to you?

Ivy.   He asked my mother to take Cliff into another
room and begged me to come home. He
actually pleaded with me to come back to
him again.

Dr. G. What did you tell him?

Ivy.   I told him I wasn't coming home, and that I
had to go to Toronto to see my friend
Cathy, so he shouldn't try to contact me
for a few days.

Chester left the house on Chester Street, feeling sad and
rejected.

Dr. G. What happened next?

Ivy.   Jake is going to pick me up early this evening
and take me to the high school so I can go
swimming.

I next progressed Grace to her rendezvous with Jake. She
told me that she saw Chester when she was leaving the Tourist
Hotel, so she ditched him and rented a room on Purdy Street
(the Purdy Street apartment). When Ivy's description of the
ensuing conversation began, I noted her expression change
suddenly and her voice deepen as she spoke Jake's part of the
dialogue as well as Grace's.

Grace. Where have you been? I've been waiting
here in the street for fifteen minutes.

Jake.   Sorry, doll, I had an errand to run. Hop in.

Grace. I saw my idiot husband not far from here,
looking for me. Let's go. I got us a place

> on Purdy Street for tonight and as long as
> we want.

Jake. What time did you say you want me to pick
you up?

Grace. Nine-thirty. Be there no later than nine-
thirty and wait for me. What are you going
to do while I'm swimming?

Jake. First, I have to get some money from a guy
who owes me. Then I'll get a drink while
my little mermaid gets her tail wet. (Laugh-
ter.)

Jake dropped Grace off at the high school, and she went
swimming. A couple of hours later, Jake returned to pick her up.
He looked like he'd had more than a few drinks.

Grace. Jake, how many drinks did you have?

Jake. I don't know. What difference does it make?

Grace. You know, honey, it's going to be great living together. We'll be like a family.

Jake. Yeah, the both of us are quite a pair.

Grace. And don't forget Cliff.

Jake. What? Who said anything about Cliff?

Grace. But, baby, I thought you would have figured that Cliff will be living with us. You
don't think I'm going to let that idiot Chester raise him. He's only three, you know.

Jake. Nah, I figured you'd dump the brat with your
mother. Now, I'm pissed. Hey, listen, I
have to get some stuff from my place first.

Ivy. But that's in North Tonawanda.

> Jake. It's not that far. With this buggy, we'll be at Purdy Street in no time.

Jake was quick to anger even when he wasn't drinking, and during the drive their discussion rapidly escalated into a heated argument.

> Jake. You know what the guys were talking about at the bar? I had to hear about all the men you've slept with. I hear you're still sleeping around.

> Grace. Who told you that?

> Jake. The bartender. He knows you pretty well. He tells me you've been there with a couple of other guys just recently.

> Grace. That's a lie.

> Jake. And they all talk about how you dress—look at that outfit you're wearing.

> Grace. What about it? I bought this just for you. You always said I look good when I wear red. That's why I picked these shoes and....

> Jake. I think you look like a cheap tart right now.

> Grace. And I think you're drunk, probably too drunk to show me a good time tonight. (Mocking laughter.)

Without warning, Jake punched her with his right hand, square on her jaw. She was conscious but in pain.

> Grace. What are you stopping for, you bastard?

> Jake. I'm going to teach you not to laugh at me. I'm going to teach you real good.

> Dr. G. Grace, what is going on?

Ivy.   It's Jake. He's crazy. He's beating me. He's stabbing me with a knife...my throat...he's
strangling me.

Jake strangled Grace, beating her badly until she died. I
guided her to the superconscious mind level.

Dr. G.   What happened, Grace?

Ivy.   I just can't believe it. That animal stabbed me
and strangled me and beat me and threw
me into Ellicott Creek. I fought like hell,
but I was no match for him.

Dr. G.   Grace, do you know Jake in your current
life as Ivy?

Ivy.   Yes, he's John.

It seems that it took re-living this life to deal with Ivy's neck
phobia. It must have removed some slight remaining karmic debt
with John that I was unaware of. Shortly after this regression, Ivy
lost her fear concerning turtlenecks. Dave could touch her neck
without Ivy exhibiting any kind of phobic reaction.

I noted that Ivy had progressed enough that it was not
necessary for Dave to be present in this life, but I was somewhat
surprised that neither Chester nor Cliff showed up in her current
life. Grace's mother is her sister in this lifetime, but nobody else
from that life is in her present life.

Another interesting aspect of this life was Grace's fascination with water. It is ironic that she was killed right after going
swimming, and then dumped into a creek. We must also note a
correspondence in John's name being Jake in this life, reminis-
cent of his life as Jakub, when he drowned Ivy as Sophia, the
Polish pianist.

This life left me with a last thought on the nature of karma.
According to the Buffalo Police Department, this is still an
unsolved murder; when I described this case to a colleague, she

asked me if John could be prosecuted for Grace's murder. Although there is no statute of limitation on murder, the karmic system is a far better source of justice than any legal system that has ever been devised by man.

I have to wonder if the subconscious force that motivated Ivy so strongly to want be regressed into this life had to do with the deep synchronicity that brought us together, and brought her story through me to CBS, and thus to the public at large. Perhaps Grace Doze's unhappy spirit could not rest without clearing up the mystery of her death.

At any rate, I later realized that Ivy had given me something I had never run into in my curiosity about documenting past lives. This last regression, at first glance, seemed similar to many others I conducted with Ivy. The big difference was that it provided a full name, Grace Doze, a place, Buffalo, New York, and the date of her death, May 17, 1927. Due to this relatively recent date and the fact that it occurred in a metropolitan area, and in a manner so sensational, if there had been a real Grace Doze, there had to be public records. Though it didn't occur to me at the time, I had finally been given the material to thoroughly document a past-life regression.

12: DOCUMENTATION

It should be pointed out at this time that I did not set out initially to document any of Ivy's lives. My practice is a clinical one, not research oriented. When I conduct a past-life regression, I don't care much about names, dates and places because they are not of therapeutic value. It was pure luck—if there is such a thing as luck—that the name Doze was mentioned when Ivy referred to her husband as "Chester, the boring, Doze." It wasn't until I chanced to go over the transcripts nearly three years after I completed my treatment of Ivy that I attempted to research the name Grace Doze.

When I verified that she had actually existed and recalled the literal accuracy of some of Ivy's statements, I went back to my notes to explore her other regressions more thoroughly. A casual examination of historical references I had on hand convinced me that there was a pattern of factual basis throughout Ivy's case history. When I reviewed the final regression I was struck by the wealth of physical detail it contained. It was only then that I determined to pursue an investigation.

I had assumed that Grace's death would have been reported somewhere. In 1927, of course, there was no television, and radio was an infant industry. So my first step was to contact the local city newspapers. A careful check with *The Buffalo Evening News* showed that on Saturday, May 21, 1927, the death of Grace Doze was reported. Figures 1 and 2 in the next chapter show the story as it was printed.

Remember that neither Ivy nor I nor anyone in Ivy's family or social circle had ever been to Buffalo, New York, or heard of Grace Doze—they hardly could have, as the story appeared only in Buffalo newspapers and was not reported on any wire service or through any other media.

INITIAL REPORTS

The following are word-for-word transcriptions of the original newspaper stories:

MURDERED WOMAN
IS MRS. C.G. DOZE

Husband Identifies Body Taken from Ellicott Creek as Wife, Missing from Main Street Home

The body of the murdered woman found in Ellicott Creek Wednesday morning was identified Saturday afternoon as that of Mrs. Grace Doze, Beatrice apartments, 1711 Main Street. She was 30 years old.

The first identification was made by Mrs. Frances Newkirk, 179 High Street, a friend. Later, Mrs. Doze's husband, Chester G. Doze, identified the body at the county morgue. A news reporter had informed Doze at his home that the body at the morgue was that of his wife. While they were conversing a deputy sheriff arrived and took the husband to the sheriff's office and later to the morgue.

The murdered woman's mother, Mrs. Marion Loveless, of 225 Chester Street, had been brought to the sheriff's office. She brought along the 3-year-old son of the dead woman. The mother is about 60 years old and lives in a small cottage on Chester Street. Her husband, a marine engineer at present, is living in Newark, New Jersey.

Meets Husband at Home

A News reporter called at the Beatrice apartments, shortly after the identification had been made by Mrs. Newkirk. There was no response to a ring at the bell of the apartment occupied by the

Doze family. The reporter started to walk up the stairs to the upper apartment. As he did so, the street door opened and a man entered.

The man said he was Chester Doze and that his wife had not been home for about a week.

"She's in Toronto" said Doze, standing in the doorway, smoking a cigarette. "Why, what's the trouble?"

"Don't you know that she has been connected with this murder along Ellicott Creek?"

"What murder do you mean?" queried Doze, taking a hasty puff at the cigarette, and shooting the butt away.

He was told of the finding of the woman's body near Ellicott Creek.

"Well, what did she have on? Tell me that," he said, with apparent growing excitement.

"Well, one thing she had on was a pair of slippers with red heels—"

Husband Near Collapse

Doze cried out and fell forward, steadying himself with his hand on the reporter's shoulder. Then he slumped to a rocking chair in the parlor of the apartment and held his head in his hands, and crying out:

"Don't tell me that. She had those kind of shoes. Don't tell me that. Don't tell me that."

He regained some of his composure and then started to answer questions. He said that his wife had been in the habit of going out with other men and that when he remonstrated with her, she would go away and stay away two or three days.

"But she never stayed away this long," he declared.

Left Home Last Monday

He last saw her Monday. That day she went to her mother's, Mrs. Marion Loveless, 223 Chester Street. She had supper there and left the baby with her mother. She went out Monday evening, saying she was going to visit a friend, Mrs. Catherine Drago, who had visited her in Buffalo.

Doze had been working right along and had been sleeping at the apartment. But Saturday forenoon he went to his mother-in-law's and was just returning when met by the reporter. He wore his working clothes and his hands and face showed dirt from his job of cable splicer with the General Electric Company.

"What would they do that to Grace for," he sobbed. "She was a sweet-looking girl, good build. She just got going around with those other girls and they went out nights with men."

Doesn't Know Her Friends

Doze was asked if he knew any one man with whom she had been keeping company. He said that he didn't. He told of an incident when she jumped from an automobile and suffered a swollen ankle. He said she told her mother the man acted as if he were crazy.

Doze sat quiet for a few moments and then exclaimed:

"Yes, I know somebody and I'm going to get him."

A deputy sheriff came to the house and asked Doze to come with him.

Doze has been employed by the General Electric Company for about six years, he said. He became acquainted with his wife after he was discharged from the Army.

Clothes Taken Out Tuesday

Besides the shoes with the red heels, Doze said his wife had a blue suit and a beaded black dress and a tan dress and a light cream-colored hat. He came home last Tuesday noon and her clothes were still there. When he returned in the evening they were gone and he assumed that she took them for her trip to Toronto.

MRS. DOZE SLAIN
IN CITY, IS BELIEF

Girl Companion on Alleged "Parties" Is Held as Witness—Arrest of Male Suspect Expected Hourly

County authorities are now working on the theory that Mrs. Grace Doze was murdered in Buffalo Tuesday night, a short time after she left Hutchinson High school, where she had been swimming, and that her body later was thrown in Ellicott creek.

They are questioning closely Miss Margaret Whalen, 23 years old, 443 Delaware avenue, who is under arrest as a material witness in the case and expect to bring into custody, within a few hours a man who has a small business in Buffalo and who had been "on parties" with Mrs. Doze.

Medical Examiner Earl G. Danser's insistance the autopsy on the body of Mrs. Doze disclosed she had not been dead more than 12 hours, at the most, and a check-up of the time the woman left the school makes certain the fact she met with foul play soon afterward.

She was last seen Tuesday night in the pool at the school at 9:20 P.M. The lights were turned out there at 9:30 o'clock and it would not have taken her more than 15 minutes to dress, fixing the time she left the school about 9:45 P.M. The body was found in Ellicott creek at 10 A.M. next morning, slightly more than 12 hours later.

Look for Former Boxer.

Sheriff Charles F. Zimmerman and deputies Tuesday afternoon left on a mission expected to lead to important developments in the Doze case. They hinted at an arrest.

Before departing, Sheriff Zimmerman directed deputies to look for a former boxer who has been missing since the body of Mrs. Doze was identified at the morgue. The sheriff, however, does not attach any special significance to this phase of the case, it was said.

Police of the Central Park station Tuesday found a handbag on the Niagara Falls boulevard. It contained a pair of bloomers and some handkerchiefs. It may be the bag Mrs. Doze carried her clothing in when she left Hutchinson High School.

The last time Mrs. Doze, who was fond of night life, saw the man was some weeks ago when she accompanied him, two Italians and another woman who has been questioned in connection with the case, to a Niagara Street soft drink place. Persons questioned by District Attorney Guy B. Moore and Sheriff Zimmerman say this man is exceptionally strong. Strong enough to strangle a woman fighting for her life as happened to Mrs. Doze.

Another angle to the case being checked closely is the fact Mrs. Doze had made it a habit to take rides in passing automobiles to reach her destination. Her husband told authorities she was "picked up" by a man in a Ford sedan in going to school Tuesday. Whether he returned afterward to give her a ride is a question.

Jack Malone, a bartender at a saloon in Main Street, near East Ferry Street, will be questioned later in the day. He does not figure in the case except in checking Doze's statement he visited Malone the evening of the murder.

Alleged Wound To Be Examined.

Doze told Buffalo police authorities Tuesday his wife stabbed him in the arm with a pair of shears. His arm bled profusely covering an undershirt and shirt with blood. The bloody clothes were found in his home by police, and Deputy Sheriff Howard Laudan found blood stains upon a bed quilt.

Dr. Charles A. Bentz, in charge of laboratories in the City hospital, will make an examination of Doze's wound, and also obtain a sample of his blood for comparison with blood stains found on a quilt and undergarments in his home.

Doze described his home life, in detail, to Mr. Moore. It consisted of terrible quarrels when blows were exchanged and harsh words hurled back and forth, he said. Neighbors told police the couple quarreled frequently. Doze said his wife had several men friends whom he did not know and whom he saw standing on corners near his home, waiting for her. When he reproached her for allowing other men to pay her attentions, she would leave him and rent an apartment else-where, Doze said. The husband gave Mr. Moore a list of the apartments rented by his wife in various parts of the city.

Threatened To Seek Separation.

The last apartment rented by the woman was in Purdy Street near East Ferry Street. It never was occupied. Mrs. Doze was murdered by a man powerful enough to strangle her to death on the same night she rented it. At that time, she also had a room in the Tourist Hotel, Main Street and Michigan Avenue. She told her husband, after a quarrel Monday, she had decided to leave him forever and after a trip to Toronto she would get a legal separation from him.

She left her home Monday and slept at the Tourist Hotel that night. The following evening Doze met her at the home of her mother, Mrs. Mary Loveless, 225 Chester Street. With her was their three-year-old son, Chester, Jr. His wife re-fused to be reconciled and after bidding her mother and son good-bye walked out of the house saying she was going to Toronto.

Doze followed her a short distance, he told police. A block from her mother's home she engaged in conversation with a man unknown to Doze. Then they parted. The man, who was smooth-faced, gave Mrs. Doze his card. The woman then stopped at a home in Purdy Street, near East Ferry Street for some time.

When she emerged, she had made arrangements to live in the place with her son. Doze then lost track of her for some time, he said, but believing she was on her way home, he walked along Purdy Street, to East Ferry, to Michigan Avenue.

Gets Into Ford Sedan.

Doze then saw his wife standing near the office of the Cold Spring car-barns, a block from the Tourist Hotel where she had spent the previous night. When she saw him, she ran across Michigan Avenue and darted into the Tourist Hotel. Doze followed her into the hotel but could not find her, he says. He went into the hotel restaurant and ordered a cup of coffee.

With the cup in his hand he went to a window facing on Main Street. At that moment his wife was getting into a Ford sedan on Main Street, across from the hotel. As Doze watched, the car sped forth. This was at 7:45 o'clock, Tuesday evening, Doze told authorities.

He next went home and changed from his working clothes into another suit. He sought the companionship of a bartender in a Main Street cafe, but found the bartender-friend not interested. Then he went home to sleep, he says.

These elements of the stories confirm statements made by Ivy as Grace Doze:

1. The body of Grace Doze was found in Ellicott Creek.

2. The murder occurred in the spring of 1927, specifically May 17, 1927.

3. Grace's home address was stated as 1711 Main Street. She referred to her home as the "Main Street apartment."

4. The name of Grace's husband was Chester, and he worked for General Electric.

5. Grace's mother lived on Chester Street.

6. Grace's maiden name was Loveless.

7. She had a three-year-old son.

8. Grace Doze told Chester Doze on May 17 that she was on her way to Toronto.

9. Grace was found with two-toned shoes, specifically with red heels.

10. Chester Doze confirmed that he saw Grace on Monday, May 16, 1927.

11. Chester Doze also confirmed the fact that Grace saw other men.

12. Grace was seen swimming at Hutchinson High School on Tuesday, May 17, 1927, and left the building at 9:45 p.m.

13. The medical examiner, Earl G. Danser, confirmed that Grace died on Tuesday, May 17, 1927, at about 10 p.m. and was strangled and beaten to death by a strong man.

14. Grace was known to "take rides in passing automobiles." She was seen being "picked up by a man in a Ford sedan."

15.   Chester Doze stated that Grace recently "stabbed him in the arm with a pair of shears."

16.   Chester stated that he and his wife argued often and physically attacked each other. Neighbors also confirmed the quarreling.

17.   Chester saw Grace's lovers "standing on corners near his home waiting for her." He also stated that Grace rented various apartments for her liaisons.

18.   Chester admitted that Grace told him she was leaving him forever on Monday, May 16, 1927, the day before she died.

19.   Chester told the reporter that he met with Grace at his mother-in-law's home on Chester Street on Tuesday, May 17, and their son was there. Chester tried to reconcile with Grace but his pleas were rejected.

OTHER REPORTS OF GRACE'S MURDER

The Buffalo Courier Express on May 19, 1927, described the details of the murder as follows:

An unusual pair of black patent leather, one-strap oxfords, size four, with a red design and an all-red heal marked Artist Style is the means by which authorities hope to identify the body of a handsome bob-haired woman found floating in Ellicott Creek, near the Lehigh Valley Bridge.

The woman had been strangled to death and her body thrown into the creek. Two superficial stab wounds under her chin, one about an inch long and the other about one-half inch long, both indicative of the murderous assault perpetrated on the woman was discovered by Medical Examiner Earl G. Danser when he performed an autopsy at the morgue.

The autopsy conclusively revealed two important facts. The first was that the woman had been strangled and that she was dead before being thrown in the water.

The medical examiner also declared that there is no question but that the woman was stabbed before she was strangled, which indicates, he said, that she struggled when the knife, believed to have been a pen-knife, was wielded on her face. The bruises, Dr. Danser asserted, were undoubtedly received in the struggle.

The Saturday, May 21, 1927, edition of *The Buffalo Evening News* reported thus:

Possibility that the identity of the beautiful young woman, whose body was found in Ellicott Creek Wednesday, never will be known, was seen by authorities today with the announcement that practically every promising clue has been exhausted without revealing a trace of the girl's identity.

If she is not identified today, it is almost certain that the seemingly impenetrable mystery will be buried with her. The body is decaying rapidly, and if someone does not recognize her within the next 12 hours, identification will be next to impossible.

Initials L.J.S.

One or two leads are being investigated, but they furnish only a slim chance that the beautiful young victim will be identified. One is a peculiar set of initials, believed to be L.J.S. on the lining of a small vest pocket on the left breast of the suit coat. The initials are machine attached, but amateurish. Authorities hope that any person, reading of the initials in the newspapers, may come to the morgue and divulge whatever information they may possess. It would be impossible to trace anyone through the initials unless the information was advanced.

The girl was dressed in a blue serge suit, with short skirt. The coat is double-breasted, with red taping around the collar, cuffs, lapel and two outside pockets. The pocket on which the initials were found was gray, but the other pockets and the sleeves are lined with red cloth.

She wore patent leather black oxfords with one strap, with a red design at the instep and red heels. They were size four. On the instep in gilded letters were the words "Artist Style." She also was clad in a wine-colored shirtwaist, light-colored stockings, and neat but inexpensive underclothing. She had dark brown hair, recently cut in a boyish bob style, and she weighed about 145 pounds.

Here we have numerous confirmations of what Ivy said in trance. The description of her clothes, especially the shoes with the red heels, and the recent haircut match perfectly. I can suggest no speculation on the mysterious initials, except to wonder if the "J" might stand for Jake. The body was not identified as that of Grace Doze until Saturday, May 21, 1927, at about 3:35 p.m.

On June 1, *The Buffalo Courier Express* reported the following:

> A small black suitcase owned by Mrs. Grace Doze and carried by her the night she was thrown into the Ellicott Creek, town of Tonawanda, yesterday was located by Detective Sergeant James E. Quigley, head of the homicide squad.
>
> The suitcase, which contained a green bathing suit, black beaded dress, lingerie, two towels, and a pocketbook, has been in the possession of police since last Wednesday, but was not examined until yesterday when Chester Doze, husband of the murdered woman, was shown the articles and identified the bag and contents as the property of his wife.
>
> The suitcase and contents showed unmistakable marks of having been in water. It is believed that it was found in the canal by somebody who threw it on the bank without opening the suitcase.

Again, this corroborates Ivy's description.

Figure 5 shows a photo of one Eleanor McCormick, originally thought by police, and even some relatives, to be the victim. Ms. McCormick apparently looked a lot like Grace Doze, whom all reports describe as a notably attractive young lady. Nonetheless, a strange anonymity seems to have attached itself to this young woman-about-town.

The Buffalo Courier Express on May 20, 1927, reported the following in reference to Grace's then unidentified body in the morgue:

> Robert George, attendant at the morgue, said it was remarkable how many persons viewed the body and declared the face to be familiar. He said the girl had evidently been in a position where she met people, as numerous ones claim to have seen her before, although none could name her.

Even anonymous in death, Grace remained memorable.

POLICE RECORDS

The Buffalo Police Department has no records dating back to 1927. But a check with the Tonawanda Police Department revealed the following surviving records from an old police blotter:

WEDNESDAY, MAY 18, 1927

10:45 A.M. Report body of young woman floating in Ellicott Creek.

A call was received from the Tonawanda City Police, saying that the body of a young girl about 17 years of age had been found floating in Ellicott

Creek near the L.V.R.R. bridge. They said that one of their officers was there and would stay until our men arrived. Chief Mang was notified and went at once to investigate. I also sent Officer McCadden, and notified the Medical Examiner's office and they said that Dr. Long would attend the call.

Lieut. Eggleston.

2:20 P.M. Report on finding of woman's body in Ellicott Creek.

Chief Mang reports that the woman found floating in Ellicott Creek near the Kibler farm was apparently murdered before she was thrown in the water. The body was found by Mrs. Bertha Tunmore, who lives on the old Kibler farm on Ellicott Creek Road. Mrs. Tunmore stopped a passing autoist who was Officer Marone of the Tonawanda City Police. Marone notified Tonawanda Police and they in turn notified us. Chief Mang and Officer McCadden responded at once. The woman was about 25 or 30 years of age, 5 feet 6 inches tall, weight about 140 pounds, black hair, fair complexion. She wore a blue serge suit with a red front in the waist, gray silk hose, black and red high heel slippers. Dr. Earl G. Danser, who took charge of the case instead of Medical Examiner Long, said that it was a case of the woman being dead before she was put in the water.

Chief Mang is investigating the case and trying to identify the woman. (She had bobbed hair.) The woman had two stab wounds on the left side of the neck and chin, which had fresh blood on them.

Lieut. Eggleston.

THURSDAY, MAY 19, 1927

10:30 A.M. Woman found in Ellicott Creek identified by brothers.

I called the County Morgue and found that the young woman who was found murdered in Ellicott Creek May 18 had just been identified by her brothers. She was Elinore McCormick of 1569 Seneca Street, Buffalo, N.Y. She was 23 years of age. She had been staying at Niagara Falls, N.Y. I was unable to get her address at the Falls.
Lieut. Eggleston.

2:10 P.M. Identification of woman was in error. The real Eleanor McCormick was located at Niagara Falls, N.Y. where she has been working.

A call was received from the City Editor's office of The Buffalo Times saying that the identification of the woman found in Ellicott Creek yesterday which was made by the McCormick brothers this morning was an error. The real Eleanor McCormick was located at 609 Erie Street, Niagara Falls, N.Y. where she was working, and that she was on her way to Buffalo now. I called the Medical Examiner's office and was told that Miss Eleanor McCormick had just arrived from the Falls and that they had no information up to this time as to who the woman was who was found murdered. They said that another brother and a sister viewed the body after the two brothers had identified it as her and told them of the error before they found Eleanor at the Falls.

Lieut. Eggleston.

8:00 P.M. Knife found at Ellicott Creek.

Call from Tonawanda Police saying that Officer Marohn had found a knife with blade open at the intersection of Colvin Blvd. and Ellicott Creek which is about 1/2 mile from where girl's body was found in the creek. Chief Mang turned the knife over to Under-Sheriff Schwindler.

Hambleton.

SATURDAY, MAY 21, 1927

3:35 P.M. Woman who was murdered identified by friend.

A call was received from the Buffalo Evening News reporter saying that the woman who was murdered and found in Ellicott Creek May 19, 1927, had just been identified by a friend by the name of Mrs. Mabel Newkirk, as Mrs. Grace Doze, of 1711 Main Street, Buffalo, N.Y., the Beatrice Apts. Age 30 years. She is married and has one child. She was not living with her husband. After the identification it was found that she has been staying at 225 Chester Street, Buffalo, N.Y. She was with Mrs. Newkirk Tuesday afternoon, May 17, and had an appointment with her for Wednesday afternoon which she did not keep. I called the Medical Examiner's office and verified the identification. They said that the Sheriff's office was trying to locate her husband at this time.

Lieut. Eggleston.

1977 FEATURE STORY

If this isn't enough to convince even the most skeptical, there is more. Figure 3 shows an article in the magazine section of *The Buffalo Evening News* dated May 21, 1977, and transcribed here:

IN A QUIRK OF HISTORY, HEADLINE UNRAVELS MAN'S 50-YEAR MYSTERY

He has lived with the image for 50 years—a child's misty recollection of his mother leaving a house on Chester St.

"She said she was going to get me an ice cream cone," Clifford C. Doze remembers. "She never came back."

He was 3 then, too young to comprehend why his relatives seldom talked about his mother.

"I can remember the door on Chester St. and wanting to follow her so bad. I didn't want to be left there. I watched the door for the longest time...."

That was in May 1927. It was years before anyone told him his mother was dead, more years before he suspected there was something dark and tragic about her death.

Now, at 53, Clifford Doze knows the truth—or as much of the truth as any person still alive can know.

His mother was murdered.

That he knows it, even now, is due to an accident of history. While the world was enthralled with Charles Lindbergh's flight to Paris in 1927, ordinary people continued to live and die.

Two of these people were Chester and Grace Doze, Clifford's parents. Chester Doze was a cable splicer. Grace liked to swim and didn't like being tied down.

"I can remember a lot of yelling and hollering around the house," Chester and Grace Doze's only child said as he poked into memories of long ago.

Newspaper reports of the time confirm Mr. Doze's recollections of his parents' home life: "It consisted of terrible quarrels when blows were exchanged and harsh words hurled back and forth."

Mrs. Doze once stabbed her husband in the arm with a pair of shears. She threatened repeatedly to leave him.

On the morning of Wednesday, May 18, 1927, a young woman was found strangled and beaten to death in Ellicott Creek near Colvin Ave. in the Town of Tonawanda. She was wearing a blue dress and black and red shoes. Police believed she had been tossed down the creek bank from a car.

"She had a thin face with small and regular features," according to a newspaper account that told how 200 persons viewed the unidentified body in the morgue. "Her hair was worn in a boyish bob."

The following Saturday, a neighbor said the victim was Grace Doze. The same day Chester Doze identified the corpse as that of his 30-year-old wife.

It was a Page One story that May 21, 1927. But the banner headline in *The Buffalo Evening News* read, "Lindbergh in France."

The 3-year-old Clifford knew none of this. His grandmother, Mrs. Marion Loveless, the mother of the victim, took him into her home on Chester Ave.

The Chester St. house (from which Clifford Doze had seen his mother walk away forever) was nearly as familiar to the child as his parents' Main St. apartment.

Police questioned the victim's husband. He told the sad story of a marriage that had disintegrated in jealousy, accusations, drinking and violence.

A newspaper account said Chester Doze fought with his wife the Monday before her body was found.

"The following evening Doze met her at the home of her mother... With her was their 3-year-old son... His wife refused to be reconciled and after bidding her mother and son good-bye she walked out of the house...."

If the newspaper account was accurate, that was the last time Clifford Doze saw his mother. It was Tuesday, May 17, 1927. Police knew Grace Doze went to a swimming class at Hutchinson High School the same night.

The next morning she was found in the creek.

A number of men and women who had known Mrs. Doze were interrogated. So, of course, was Chester Doze. The killing was never solved.

"My grandmother just told me she was gone," Clifford Doze said.

Chester Doze remarried. One day, when Clifford was 10 or 11, his stepmother said something about "going over to the cemetery to put flowers on the grave," Clifford Doze said.

Another time, when Clifford misbehaved, his stepmother blurted, "You're going to wind up like your mother," he remembers.

But none of his parents' relatives would tell him the truth: "It seemed to be a taboo subject all the while I was growing up."

The grandmother who largely raised him dropped a different secret accidentally: Grace Doze had been married before her unhappy match to Chester.

The first union bore a son, Clifford Doze's half-brother, who died before Clifford was born.

As the years went by, there were fewer and fewer persons who could have told Clifford Doze about his mother.

"The old man, he never said a word. Of course, he was pretty close-mouthed anyhow," Clifford Doze said.

Chester Doze died several years ago in his 60s. His second wife has also died.

On May 21, Clifford Doze was sitting in his home at 518 LaSalle Ave., relaxing with that day's Buffalo Evening News.

The front of the Magazine section bore a re-creation of the front page of The Buffalo Evening News of May 21, 1927, in honor of the 50th anniversary of Lindbergh's flight.

Clearly visible in the upper left corner of the reproduction was the headline "Murdered Woman is Mrs. C.G. Doze."

And with that headline, 50 years of secrecy were wiped away for Clifford Doze.

Now, as before, his feeling about his parents are a mixture of detachment and compassion: "I don't judge them. I feel they've both been judged."

Blunt-spoken but friendly, Mr. Doze is an exterminator. He and his wife, Ethel, have three daughters and like to get away from the world's sorrows by taking boat trips around the Great Lakes.

He's glad to know the truth, finally, and talked about what happened a half-century ago without apparent reluctance: "Everybody that could have been hurt by that is dead now."

Mr. Doze has never seen his mother's grave but he said he may search it out. Chester and Grace Doze are both buried in Forest Lawn—apart in death as they were in life.

This article provides further corroboration of statements made by Ivy:

1.   Though in initial accounts Grace's son is referred to as Chester, Jr., this article consistently refers to Grace's son as Clifford.

2.   Cliff confirms being at his grandmother's home on Chester Street on May 17, 1927, the day his mother was murdered.

3.   Grace was found on May 18, 1927, wearing a blue dress and black-and-red shoes.

4.   Cliff stated that he spent a lot of time with his grandmother on Chester Street.

5.   Cliff stated that his grandmother informed him of Grace's previous marriage and a child by her first husband, who died before Clifford was born.

It is most significant that Ivy's statements in trance in several details reflect an accurate knowledge of information–such as her age and the correct name of her son–apparently unavailable even to contemporary news reporters and police investigators.

GRACE DOZE'S DEATH CERTIFICATE

In Figure 4, you can see that Grace's death certificate was issued on May 23, 1927, six days after her death. From the certificate we see that her body was found in Ellicott Creek in Tonawanda on May 18, 1927. Her date of birth was January 11, 1895, which confirms statements Ivy made to me about being thirty years old in 1925. This document also states that she was a housewife and that her maiden name was Loveless, and confirms the fact that Grace's mother lived on Chester Street. In addition, the cause of death is listed as Asphyxia by Strangulation, which corresponds with Ivy's trance description of her death.

GRACE'S FATAL RIDE.

According to Buffalo's medical examiner, Earl G. Danser, Grace Doze died between 10:00 p.m. and midnight on the night of May 17, 1927. From what Ivy told me in trance, Jake picked her up at about 9:30 p.m. The distance between Hutchinson Technical High School (called John F. Kennedy Recreation Center today—see Figure 6) and Ellicott Creek near Colvin Avenue is eight miles.

Figure 7 shows the path Jake and Grace took on that fatal evening. Arrow #1 indicates the location of Hutchinson Technical High School. The location of Ellicott Creek where Grace's body was found is indicated by Arrow #2. The fact that it is only eight miles between these two locations makes it quite plausible for Grace to have been killed between 10:00 p.m. and midnight. This route is also consistent with Grace and Jake being on their way to Jake's place in North Tonawanda.

Subsequent research has shown that Ellicott Creek was a bad part of town, notorious for prostitutes, drug dealers, and other unsavory characters, where corpses were not uncommon during this era. It would have been a likely place for someone connected with the underworld—a bootlegger like Jake—to dispose of a body.

GRACE'S RESIDENCES

Figure 8 (Arrow #1) shows the location of the Tourist Hotel (Main Street and Michigan Avenue) where Grace spent the night on Monday, May 16, 1927, after she told Chester Doze she was leaving him for good.

The last time Chester and Cliff spoke to Grace was at the home of Grace's mother, on Chester Street, indicated by Arrow #2.

The Purdy Street apartment, located at the intersection of Purdy Street and East Ferry Street, which Grace rented on Tuesday, May 17, 1927 (the last day of her life), and where she planned to live with Jake, is indicated by Arrow #3.

Arrow #4 shows the location of the apartment where Grace, Chester and Cliff lived. The address of this residence was 1711 Main Street.

GRACE'S FLAPPER FRIEND

Grace and her friends typified the Roaring Twenties' "liberated" flapper image—party girls who thumbed rides and attended speakeasies together. Grace made references to wild times with her friend, Mary, and, in fact, used the name Margaret Carter on the last day of her life when she registered at the Tourist Hotel, and at the Purdy Street apartments. Carter was the last name of Grace's first husband, no longer living in 1927.

Miss Margaret E. Whalen, age 23, of 443 Delaware Avenue (a short walk from Grace's Main street apartment,) was mentioned in numerous newspaper articles. (See Figures 9 and 10.) She was always a reluctant witness and never gave the authorities any information about Jake. She did describe the parties she and Grace attended, as reported in the *Buffalo Courier Express* on May 27:

Miss Margaret Whalen also was examined, the questioning being confined chiefly to the details of a party which took place in a Glenwood Avenue apartment April 20. The apartment was rented by Mrs. Doze. The latter and Miss Whalen are said to have entertained three men there and the county authorities desired to know their identity.

Miss Whalen said much liquor was consumed during the party and she was intoxicated when she left the apartment. Two of the men left with her, she said, and she finally slipped away from them and went to her home in Delaware Avenue. The third man remained in the apartment with Mrs. Doze. Miss Whalen told Sheriff Zimmerman she did not know the names of any of the men. She had not since seen them, she said.

On May 24, *The Buffalo Evening Times* reported:

Miss Whalen was taken into custody last night. Sheriff Zimmerman contends the girl knows the identity of the auto mechanic sought in connection with the slaying, although she denied this. Sheriff Zimmerman said he learned that Miss Whalen and Mrs. Doze had been on "wild parties" on several occasions and also that they had roomed together one time when Mrs. Doze quarreled with her husband.

(The auto mechanic was subsequently dropped as a suspect.)

Margaret Whalen "would not reveal the names of any of the men who accompanied herself and Mrs. Doze on parties." *The Buffalo Evening News* (figure 10) stated on May 26, "Thus far, Miss Whalen has maintained a silence regarding persons who might throw light on the murder."

Though Prohibition was not widely respected legislation during this era, the speakeasy world was still an underworld. If the girls socialized with bootleggers and other criminal types they were likely involved with the Mafia, then at the height of its activities locally. (As late as July 26, 1936, the *Buffalo Courier Express* ran the headline, "Mafia Code Seen As Big Factor in Mystery Killings.") The Mafia's "code of silence" was well known in 1927. Margaret Whalen might most definitely fear for her life if she talked to the police.

CHESTER DOZE

On May 23, 1927, *The Buffalo Evening News* ran a story with Chester Doze's photo (Figure 11). This article is also significant in that it verifies Grace's attendance at her swimming class at Hutchinson Central Technical High School.

County officers Monday afternoon centered their investigation into the murder of Mrs. Grace Doze, whose body was found in Ellicott Creek Wednesday morning, in an effort to determine the movements of the young wife after she left Hutchinson Central High School, where she was known to have been up to 9:30 o'clock Tuesday night.

That she was at the high school and attended a swimming class there was revealed to Sheriff Zimmerman and his investigators Monday by John K. Wolf, superintendent of swimming in the public schools and Miss Carlotta C. Boll, swimming instructor at Central-Hutchinson.

Mrs. Doze attended regularly the Tuesday evening swimming classes and was there the night she was last seen alive, according to the statements of Superintendent Wolf and Miss Bolls. The names of others who attended the class have been given to Sheriff Zimmerman and they will all be questioned, it was said.

The Buffalo Courier Express, on May 22, showed a photo of Chester leaving City Hall (Figure 12). Also in this edition is a photo of Clifford Doze at age 3, whom the paper incorrectly refers to as Chester, Jr. This article states:

"He was in no shape to make a real statement," said the sheriff, "so we only asked him a few questions and had him outline his end of the case."

According to a report at the Sheriff's office, Doze has altered several of his original statements. He now holds it is said "that his last sight of his wife was when he saw her step from a side entrance of the Tourist Hotel, Main and Michigan Avenue, and enter a light closed car in which she was driven away towards the business district of the city. A man about 43 years old who wore glasses was at the wheel of the car," he said.

Doze has declared, according to the report, that he was seated at a table in a nearby restaurant and caught only a glimpse of his wife as she sped across the street. He qualified this statement later, however, it is said, when he declared he saw her pause in the center of the street and hail a number of cars passing in a southerly direction. The car she finally stepped into, he was said to have told Sheriff Zimmerman, might have been stopped in recognition of her signal that she desired a lift downtown. He did not obtain the license number of the car and he did not recognize the man at the wheel, it is said Doze told the sheriff.

Chester Doze is employed as a cable splicer by the Buffalo General Electric Company. He formerly was a professional boxer, fighting under the ring name of "Kid Doze."

The Buffalo Courier Times on May 24, 1927, reported the following about Chester Doze's statement to the police:

During the grilling a man's bloody shirt, which local detectives found in his apartment at 1711 Main Street, was taken to the district attorney's office. The police at first believed the shirt was an important clue. Doze, however, explained the garment was one he had worn on a night several weeks ago when he was stabbed in the left arm by his wife with a small pair of scissors during one of their frequent domestic arguments.

Doze bared his arm and showed his interrogators the wound inflicted by his wife. Dr. McClure of the city health department was called to examine the wound and pronounced that it had been suffered at least two weeks ago. Mr. Moore, however, stated he would have a blood examination made to verify the doctor's report.

> It was brought out during the questioning of Doze that he was unable to read or write. This was revealed when Mr. Moore requested him to read over portions of the statement he was making. "I can only read a little, just short words," was the reply of Doze. He then further admitted that he barely could write.

The stabbing of Chester by Grace was estimated to have occurred no sooner than May 10. This coincides within in a few days with what Ivy told me.   Also, Chester's illiteracy would explain Grace's constant reference to him as the "idiot."

The Buffalo Courier Express reported on May 23 that:

> It developed from statements taken from Doze that he and his wife parted Monday night after a quarrel involving her alleged intimacy with other men. She left her home in anger, Doze told the sheriff, and said she was going to her mother's house.
>
> Doze remained home that evening, but on Tuesday night he visited his mother-in-law's home and found his wife. He attempted to effect a reconciliation, but Mrs. Doze refused to talk to him. He left while she was conversing with her mother.
>
> Doze learned that his wife had not stayed at her mother's house Monday night but had registered at a Main Street hotel as Margaret Carter. Tuesday night he followed her from her mother's home and followed her into the Tourist Hotel. Again he pleaded with her to return home but she spurned him, he told the sheriff, and replied she was going to visit a girlfriend in Toronto, Mrs. Catherine Drago, 801-1/2 College. While he was

talking with her, she left the hotel and entered an automobile at the curb. The machine went south on Main Street. That was the last time Doze saw his wife alive.

Doze said they were married seven years ago in Buffalo. Until a year ago, they lived with Mrs. Loveless at the Chester Street address, when they moved to the Beatrice apartments in Main St. Two of their children died, but the second child, Chester, Jr., three years old, has lived with them until they separated last Monday.

"I read the newspaper accounts of that terrible murder but I never thought the victim was my poor Grace," Doze said between sobs. "I can see it all now, those red shoes that the people spoke so much about. She bought them only two days before she left me, and her clothing was the same she wore when we had that last quarrel."

This also confirms the fact that Grace and her family lived with Marion Loveless at 225 Chester Street until 1926, and that Grace lost at least two other children. Chester also confirmed the fact that Grace bought the shoes with the red heels on Saturday, May 14.

This same edition reported that:

The county authorities believe Mrs. Doze had no intention of going to Toronto Tuesday, but told her mother of her proposed visit so she would not worry.

Mrs. Doze had arranged an appointment for Tuesday night and kept the tryst. The man with whom she went out is the person who killed her and threw her body in the creek, in the opinion of the officers.

Another interesting finding in this case was reported in *The Buffalo Evening Times* on May 23:

> Chester Doze, 1711 Main Street, husband of Mrs. Grace Doze, found strangled in Ellicott Creek a week ago last Wednesday will be questioned about a suit of men's clothing found in his apartment Friday which appears to be several sizes too large for him, according to Sheriff Charles F. Zimmerman. The suit was made for a man weighing upwards of 200 pounds, while Doze weighs only 150 pounds, according to the sheriff. The coat of the suit is brown with a green stripe, navy blue trousers and blue vest.

Jake was tall and strong. Apparently he had changed clothes in Grace's apartment at one of their liaisons.

GRACE'S BIRTH CERTIFICATE

From this document (Figure 16), we note that Grace was born on January 21, 1895. This is ten days later than the date that appears on her death certificate (see Figure 4). It is ironic that she was raised at 39 Chester Street and that her parents later moved to 225 Chester Street. The name Chester was to haunt Grace throughout her life.

CLIFFORD C. DOZE'S BIRTH CERTIFICATE

Clifford C. Doze was born on November 22, 1923 (Figure 15). From this document we see that Grace had three children who died (item number 20). Ivy, in trance, stated she lost two other sons. I could not find any documents to identify Grace's other children by name. Perhaps two of these three children were boys.

GRACE'S MOTHER—MARION LOVELESS

The Buffalo Courier Express on May 22 ran the following item:

> Mrs. Loveless said her daughter returned Tuesday morning and remained for luncheon. She then packed a suitcase with clothes she had left at her mother's home and announced she was going to Toronto to visit Catherine Drago, 181-1/2 College Street, that city.
>
> But Mrs. Doze apparently had no intention of going to Toronto, for she again had reserved the room at the Tourist Hotel and was seen at the hostelry at 8 o'clock Tuesday night. Deputy Sheriff Howard J. Laudam last night found the clothes Mrs. Doze had taken from her mother's home in the room she had rented at the hotel. The suitcase was not found.
>
> "I never could do anything with my daughter," Mrs. Loveless sobbed in an interview with a Buffalo Courier Express reporter. "She just

seemed to live to go out on parties. I don't think she was a bad girl, but for some strange reason home life didn't seem to satisfy her."

"We liked Chester, her husband, and seemed to think he was treating her as good as any husband could treat a wife."

Mrs. Loveless said she had done everything in her power to patch up the differences between Grace and Chester, and that Chester had at all times seemed willing to take his wife back.

"It's just something I can't understand," she said. "I thought she was safe in Toronto with her friend, Catherine Drago," Mrs. Loveless explained.

Mrs. Loveless said her daughter was married to Chester Doze about five and one-half years ago. She had been married to a man named Carter who died about seven years ago. Chester, Jr., is three-and-one-half years old.

GRACE'S GRAVE

Newspaper reports aren't always accurate. *The Buffalo Courier Express* reported on May 24, 1927, that Grace was buried in Forest Lawn Cemetery in Buffalo. Subsequent research (Figures 13 and 14), shows clearly that Grace Doze was buried at Elmlawn Memorial Gardens in Kenmore, New York. She was laid to rest in Lot No. 560, Grave No. 11.

It is interesting to note that her grave is unmarked. There is no headstone or identifying characteristic other than the burial number (10750). Just as the report of Grace's death was overshadowed by Lindbergh's landing in Paris, her burial, until now, has also been ignored.

ILLUSTRATIONS

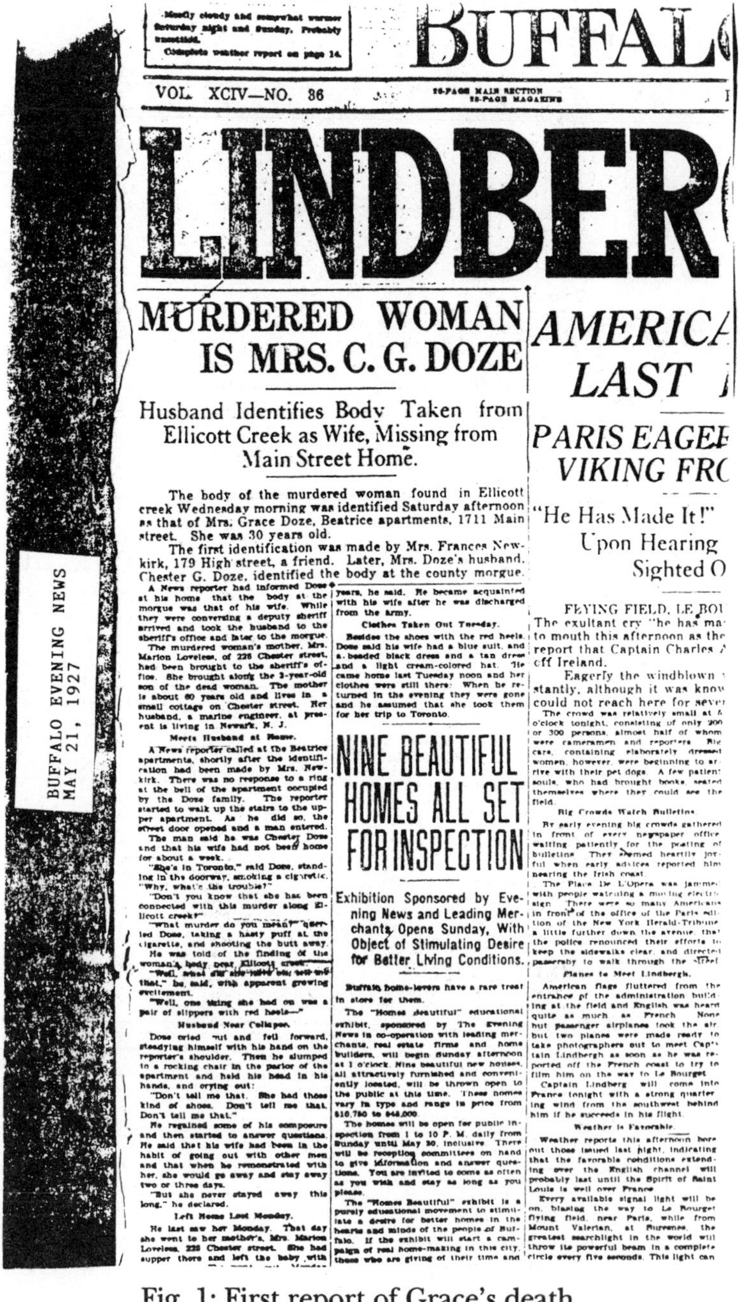

BUFFALO EVENING NEWS
MAY 21, 1927

Mostly cloudy and somewhat warmer Saturday night and Sunday. Probably unsettled.
Complete weather report on page 14.

BUFFAL

VOL. XCIV—NO. 86

16-PAGE MAIN SECTION
16-PAGE MAGAZINE

LINDBER

MURDERED WOMAN IS MRS. C. G. DOZE

Husband Identifies Body Taken from Ellicott Creek as Wife, Missing from Main Street Home.

The body of the murdered woman found in Ellicott creek Wednesday morning was identified Saturday afternoon as that of Mrs. Grace Doze, Beatrice apartments, 1711 Main street. She was 30 years old.

The first identification was made by Mrs. Frances Newkirk, 179 High street, a friend. Later, Mrs. Doze's husband, Chester G. Doze, identified the body at the county morgue.

A News reporter had informed Doze at his home that the body at the morgue was that of his wife. While they were conversing a deputy sheriff arrived and took the husband to the sheriff's office and later to the morgue.

The murdered woman's mother, Mrs. Marion Loveless, of 226 Chester street, had been brought to the sheriff's office. She brought along the 3-year-old son of the dead woman. The mother is about 60 years old and lives in a small cottage on Chester street. Her husband, a marine engineer, at present is living in Newark, N. J.

Meets Husband at Home.

A News reporter called at the Beatrice apartments, shortly after the identification had been made by Mrs. Newkirk. There was no response to a ring at the bell of the apartment occupied by the Doze family. The reporter started to walk up the stairs to the upper apartment. As he did so, the street door opened and a man entered.

The man said he was Chester Doze and that his wife had not been home for about a week.

"She's in Toronto," said Doze, standing in the doorway, smoking a cigarette. "Why, what's the trouble?"

"Don't you know that she has been connected with this murder along Ellicott creek?"

"What murder do you mean?" queried Doze, taking a hasty puff at the cigarette, and shooting the butt away.

He was told of the finding of the woman's body near Ellicott creek.

"Well, what did she have on; tell me that," he said, with apparent growing excitement.

"Well, one thing she had on was a pair of slippers with red heels—"

Husband Near Collapse.

Doze cried out and fell forward, steadying himself with his hand on the reporter's shoulder. Then he slumped to a rocking chair in the parlor of the apartment and held his head in his hands, and crying out:

"Don't tell me that. She had those kind of shoes. Don't tell me that. Don't tell me that."

He regained some of his composure and then started to answer questions. He said that his wife had been in the habit of going out with other men and that when he remonstrated with her, she would go away and stay away two or three days.

"But she never stayed away this long," he declared.

Left Home Last Monday.

He last saw her Monday. That day she went to her mother's, Mrs. Marion Loveless, 226 Chester street. She had supper there and left the baby with

years, he said. He became acquainted with his wife after he was discharged from the army.

Clothes Taken Out Tuesday.

Besides the shoes with the red heels, Doze said his wife had a blue suit, and a beaded black dress and a tan dress and a light cream-colored hat. He came home last Tuesday noon and her clothes were still there. When he returned in the evening they were gone and he assumed that she took them for her trip to Toronto.

NINE BEAUTIFUL HOMES ALL SET FOR INSPECTION

Exhibition Sponsored by Evening News and Leading Merchants Opens Sunday, With Object of Stimulating Desire for Better Living Conditions.

Buffalo home-lovers have a rare treat in store for them.

The "Homes Beautiful" educational exhibit, sponsored by The Evening News in co-operation with leading merchants, real estate firms and home builders, will begin Sunday afternoon at 1 o'clock. Nine beautiful new houses, all attractively furnished and conveniently located, will be thrown open to the public at this time. These homes vary in type and range in price from $10,750 to $48,000.

The homes will be open for public inspection from 1 to 10 P. M. daily from Sunday until May 30, inclusive. There will be reception committees on hand to give information and answer questions. You are invited to come as often as you wish and stay as long as you please.

The "Homes Beautiful" exhibit is a purely educational movement to stimulate a desire for better homes in the hearts and minds of the people of Buffalo. If the exhibit will start a campaign of real home-making in this city, those who are giving of their time and

AMERICA LAST

PARIS EAGER VIKING FRO

"He Has Made It!" Upon Hearing Sighted O

FLYING FIELD, LE BOU The exultant cry "he has ma to mouth this afternoon as the report that Captain Charles off Ireland.

Eagerly the windblown stantly, although it was know could not reach here for sever

The crowd was relatively small at 6 o'clock tonight, consisting of only 200 or 300 persons, almost half of whom were cameramen and reporters. Big cars, containing elaborately dressed women, however, were beginning to arrive with their pet dogs. A few patient souls, who had brought books, seated themselves where they could see the field.

Big Crowds Watch Bulletins.

By early evening big crowds gathered in front of every newspaper office waiting patiently for the posting of bulletins. They seemed heartily joyful when early advices reported him nearing the Irish coast.

The Place De L'Opera was jammed with people watching a moving electric sign. There were so many Americans in front of the office of the Paris edition of the New York Herald-Tribune a little further down the avenue, that the police renounced their efforts to keep the sidewalks clear, and directed passersby to walk through the street.

Planes to Meet Lindbergh.

American flags fluttered from the entrance of the administration building at the field and English was heard quite as much as French. None but passenger airplanes took the air, but two planes were made ready to take photographers out to meet Captain Lindbergh as soon as he was reported off the French coast to try to film him on the way to Le Bourget.

Captain Lindberg will come into France tonight with a strong quartering wind from the southwest behind him if he succeeds in his flight.

Weather is Favorable.

Weather reports this afternoon bore out those issued last night, indicating that the favorable conditions extending over the English channel will probably last until the Spirit of Saint Louis is well over France.

Every available signal light will be on, blazing the way to Le Bourget flying field, near Paris, while from Mount Valerian, at Suresnes, the greatest searchlight in the world will throw its powerful beam in a complete circle every five seconds. This light can

Fig. 1: First report of Grace's death.

MRS. DOZE SLAIN IN CITY, IS BELIEF

Girl Companion on Alleged "Parties" Is Held as Witness—Arrest of Male Suspect Expected Hourly.

County authorities are now working on the theory that Mrs. Grace Doze was murdered in Buffalo Tuesday night, a short time after she left Hutchinson High school, where she had been swimming, and that her body later was thrown in Ellicott creek.

They are questioning closely Miss Margaret Whalen, 23 years old, 443 Delaware avenue, who is under arrest as a material witness in the case and expect to bring into custody, within a few hours a man who has a small business in Buffalo and who had been "on parties" with Mrs. Doze.

Medical Examiner Earl G. Danser's insistence the autopsy on the body of Mrs. Doze disclosed she had not been dead more than 12 hours, at the most, and a check-up of the time the woman left the school makes certain the fact she met with foul play soon afterward.

She was last seen Tuesday night in the pool at the school at 9:20 P. M. The lights were turned out there at 9:30 o'clock and it would not have taken her more than 15 minutes to dress, fixing the time she left the school about 9:45 P. M. The body was found in Ellicott creek at 10 A. M. next morning, slightly more than 12 hours later.

Look for Former Boxer.

Sheriff Charles F. Zimmerman and deputies Tuesday afternoon left on a mission expected to lead to important developments in the Doze case. They hinted at an arrest.

Before departing, Sheriff Zimmerman directed deputies to look for a former boxer who has been missing since the body of Mrs. Doze was identified at the morgue. The sheriff, however, does not attach any special significance to this phase of the case, it was said.

Police of the Central Park station Tuesday found a handbag on the Niagara Falls boulevard. It contained a pair of bloomers and some handkerchiefs. The bag will be turned over to the sheriff. It may be the bag Mrs. Doze carried her clothing in when she left Hutchinson High school.

The last time Mrs. Doze, who was

(Continued on Page 5, Column 2)

ENGLAND TO BREAK WITH SOVIET RUSSIA

End of Diplomatic Relations Subject to House Approval, Baldwin Says.

A complete list of the new wavelength and power assignments made by the Federal Radio commission, covering every station in the country, is printed today on page 19.

WKBW ASSIGNED 217-METER WAVE WITH 500 WATTS

Federal Radio Commission, Besides Cutting Churchill Station's Power, Makes Sweeping Changes in Other Local Broadcasters Effective June 1

Sweeping changes in the wavelengths and power of Buffalo broadcasting stations are made by the Federal Radio commission in its reallocation of operating frequencies announced Tuesday in Washington. They are:

WGR, of the Federal Radio Manufacturing corporation — wavelength changed from 319 meters to 302.8 meters. Power unchanged at 750 watts.

WKBW, of the Churchill Evangelistic association—wavelength changed from 207 meters to 217.3 meters. Power reduced from 5000 watts to 500 watts. (WKBW's original license authorized power of 5000 watts. Recently it has been operating on about 1000 watts.)

WMAK, of the Norton Laboratories—wavelength changed from 400 meters to 545.1 meters. Power reduced from 1000 to 750 watts. (This latter figure has been the station's rating for several weeks.)

WEBR, of the Howell Electric company—wavelength changed from 244 meters to 241.8 meters. Power increased from 100 to 200 watts.

WSVS, Seneca Vocational school—wavelength changed from 218.8 meters to 205.4 meters. Power unchanged at 50 watts.

WPDQ, Norwood garage—wavelength

Fig. 2: Second report.

In a Quirk of History, Headline Unravels Man's 50-Year Mystery

By DAVE STOUT

He has lived with the image for 50 years — a child's misty recollection of his mother leaving a house on Chester St.

"She said she was going to get me an ice-cream cone," Clifford C. Doze remembers. "She never came back."

He was 3 then, too young to comprehend why his relatives seldom talked about his mother.

"I can remember the door on Chester St. and wanting to follow her so bad. I didn't want to be left there. I watched the door for the longest time . . ."

That was in May 1927. It was years before anyone told him his mother was dead, more years before he suspected there was something dark and tragic about her death.

NOW, AT 53, Clifford Doze knows the truth — or as much of the truth as any person still alive can know.

His mother was murdered.

That he knows it, even now, is due to an accident of history. While the world was enthralled with Charles Lindbergh's flight to Paris in 1927, ordinary people continued to live and die.

Two of these people were Chester and Grace Doze, Clifford's parents. Chester Doze was a cable splicer. Grace liked to swim and didn't like being tied down.

"I can remember a lot of yelling and hollering around the house," Chester and Grace Doze's only child said, as he poked into memories of long ago.

NEWSPAPER reports of the time confirm Mr. Doze's recollections of his parents' home life: "It consisted of terrible quarrels when blows were exchanged and harsh words hurled back and forth . . ."

Mrs. Doze once stabbed her husband in the arm with a pair of shears. She threatened repeatedly to leave him.

On the morning of Wednesday, May 18, 1927, a young woman was found strangled and beaten to death in Ellicott Creek near Colvin Ave. in the Town of Tonawanda. She was wearing a blue dress and black and red shoes. Police believed she had been tossed down the creek bank from a car.

"She had a thin face with small and regular features," according to a newspaper account that told how 200 persons viewed the unidentified body in the morgue. "Her hair was worn in a boyish bob . . ."

THE FOLLOWING Saturday, a neighbor said the victim was

CLIFFORD DOZE   50 Years of Secrecy Wiped Away

Grace Doze. The same day Chester Doze identified the corpse as that of his 30-year-old wife.

It was a Page One story that May 21, 1927. But the banner headline in The Buffalo Evening News read, "Lindbergh in France."

The 3-year-old Clifford knew none of this. His grandmother, Mrs. Marion Loveless, the mother of the victim, took him into her home on Chester Ave.

The Chester St. house (from which Clifford Doze had been his mother walk away

forever) was nearly as familiar to the child as his parents' Main St. apartment.

Police questioned the victim's husband. He told the sad story of a marriage that had disintegrated in jealousy, accusations, drinking and violence.

A NEWSPAPER account said Chester Doze fought with his wife the Monday before her body was found.

"The following evening Doze met her at the home of her mother . . . With her was their 3-year-old son . . . His wife re-

fused to be reconciled and after bidding her mother and son goodbye she walked out of the house . . ."

If the newspaper account was accurate, that was the last time Clifford Doze saw his mother. It was Tuesday, May 17, 1927. Police knew Grace Doze went to a swimming class at Hutchinson High School the same night.

The next morning she was found in the creek.

A number of men and women who had known Mrs. Doze were interrogated. So, of course, was

Chester Doze. The killing was never solved.

"My grandmother just told me she was gone," Clifford Doze said.

CHESTER DOZE remarried. One day, when Clifford was 10 or 11, his stepmother said something about "going over to the cemetery to put flowers on the grave," Clifford Doze said.

Another time, when Clifford misbehaved, his stepmother blurted, "You're going to wind up like your mother," he remembers.

But none of his parents' relatives would tell him the truth: "It seemed to be a taboo subject all the while I was growing up."

The grandmother who largely raised him dropped a different secret accidentally: Grace Doze had been married before her unhappy match to Chester.

The first union bore a son, Clifford Doze's half-brother, who died before Clifford was born.

AS THE YEARS went by, there were fewer and fewer persons who could have told Clifford Doze about his mother.

"The old man, he never said a word. Of course, he was pretty close-mouthed anyhow," Clifford Doze said.

Chester Doze died several years ago in his 60s. His second wife has also died.

On May 21, Clifford Doze was sitting in his home at 518 LaSalle Ave., relaxing with that day's Buffalo Evening News.

The front of the Magazine section bore a re-creation of the front page of The Buffalo Evening News of May 21, 1927, in honor of the 50th anniversary of Lindbergh's flight.

Clearly visible in the upper left corner of the reproduction was the headline "Murdered Woman Is Mrs. C. G. Doze."

And with that headline, 50 years of secrecy were wiped away for Clifford Doze.

NOW, AS before, his feelings about his parents are a mixture of detachment and compassion: "I don't judge them. I feel they've both been judged."

Blunt-spoken but friendly, Mr. Doze is an exterminator. He and his wife, Ethel, have three daughters and like to get away from the world's sorrows by taking boat trips around the Great Lakes.

He's glad to know the truth, finally, and talked about what happened a half-century ago without apparent reluctance: "Everybody said they should have been hurt by that is dead now."

Mr. Doze has never seen his mother's grave but he said he may search it out. Chester and Grace Doze are both buried in Forest Lawn — apart in death as they were in life.

Fig. 3: 1977 feature story.

Register of Deaths in the Town of Tonawanda, County of Erie, State of New York X33

For Genealogical Purpose Only — David L. Ulmer, Deputy Registrar

(No. Ellicott Creek ST.; WARD) Registered No. 18
(If death occurred in a hospital or institution, give its NAME instead of street and number)

FULL NAME Grace Doze

(18a) RESIDENCE No. 1711 Main ST., WARD. Buffalo, N. Y.
(Usual place of abode) (If nonresident, give city or town and State)

Length of residence in city or town where death occurred yrs. mos. ds. How long in U. S. if of foreign birth? yrs. mos. ds.

PERSONAL AND STATISTICAL PARTICULARS

SEX: Female

COLOR OR RACE: White

SINGLE, MARRIED, WIDOWED, OR DIVORCED (Write the word): Married

IF MARRIED, WIDOWED OR DIVORCED Husband of (or) Wife of: Chester Doze

DATE OF BIRTH: January 11, 1895 (Month) (Day) (Year)

AGE: 32 yrs. 4 mos. 7 ds. If LESS than 1 day, how many hrs. or min.?

OCCUPATION
(a) Trade, profession, or particular kind of work: Housewife
(b) General nature of industry, business, or establishment in which employed (or employer)
(c) Name of employer

BIRTHPLACE (City or Town) Buffalo
(State or Country) N. Y.

PARENTS

NAME OF FATHER: ~~John~~ Robert Loveless (Corrected Aug. 19 1936 by affid. of Marion K. Loveless. Letter from Dept. of Health, Aug. 7 - 1936)

BIRTHPLACE OF FATHER (City or Town) (State or Country): Michigan

MAIDEN NAME OF MOTHER: Marion Kingsford

BIRTHPLACE OF MOTHER (City or Town) (State or Country): Michigan

THE ABOVE IS TRUE TO THE BEST OF MY KNOWLEDGE
(Informant) Mrs. Marion K. Loveless
(Address) 225 Chester St. - Bflo.

Filed May 23, 1927 Roscoe F. Rosser, Registrar

MEDICAL CERTIFICATE OF DEATH

DATE OF DEATH: May 18th, 1927 (Month) (Day) (Year)

I HEREBY CERTIFY, THAT I ATTENDED DECEASED FROM After Death, 19 , TO , 19 ,

THAT I LAST SAW H ALIVE ON , 19 , AND THAT DEATH OCCURRED ON THE DATE STATED ABOVE, AT 10:30 A.M. THE CAUSE OF DEATH WAS AS FOLLOWS:

Asphyxia by Strangulation
Homicide

(DURATION) YRS. MOS. DS.

CONTRIBUTORY (Secondary)

(DURATION) YRS. MOS. DS.

WHERE WAS DISEASE CONTRACTED, IF NOT AT PLACE OF DEATH? Town of Tonawanda

DID AN OPERATION PRECEDE DEATH? DATE OF

WAS THERE AN AUTOPSY? Yes

WHAT TEST CONFIRMED DIAGNOSIS?

(SIGNED) E. G. Danser M.D.

May 21, 1927 (ADDRESS) Dep. County Physician

State the Disease Causing Death, or, in deaths from Violent Causes, State (1) Means and Nature of Injury, and (2) whether Accidental, Suicidal, or Homicidal.

PLACE OF BURIAL, CREMATION OR REMOVAL: Elmlawn

DATE OF BURIAL: May 24, 1927

UNDERTAKER: Robert E. Hennessy

ADDRESS: 2070 Niagara St.

BURIAL OR ~~TRANSIT~~ PERMIT ISSUED BY Roscoe F. Rosser DATE OF ISSUE May 23, 1927

Fig. 4: Grace's Death Certificate.

Buffl. Eve Times May 19, 1937

Buffalo Girl Found Alive After
Brother "Identifies" Body

Is A

Eleanor McC
Of Slayer
And Br
Morgue —
Unknown

The mystery su
an unidentified girl
near Colvin bouleva
McCormick, 21, who
brothers, was foun
Falls, by deputy sh
mermann's office.

The murder vic
has been in Niagara
semble ach other th
Sheriff Zimmerman
deputies had seen
Niagara Falls resta

Police of Buffa
the State have oine
girl's body was fou
the neck and throat

Fought for Life

That she put up a
before submitting to h
evident from numerou

Bride of
Annulm

Annulment of a marri
only four hours was sou
tice O'Malley in equity
preme Court today by
Kleinsmith of Forestvil
was that of a simple cou
into marriage by prom
mobiles, jewelry and a
Long Island and a sep
immediately when sh
that her husband did
money even to pay the
a wedding trip from O

ELEANOR McCORMICK

FARM RELIEF FIGHT   OLDEST MUSTACHE

Fig. 5: Look-alike Eleanor McCormick.

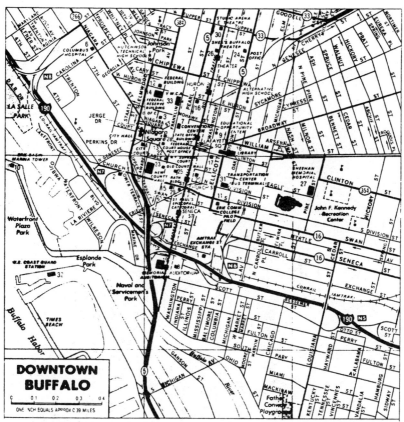

Fig.6: Hutchinson High School (swimming pool).

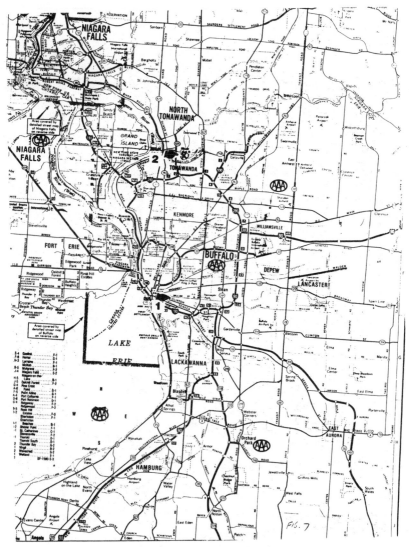

Fig. 7: Grace's fatal ride.

Fig. 8: Grace's residences.

case against proprietor of Ellicott
street store not to be
pressed

Buffalo Courier Express
May 24 1927

Held in Murder

NO EVIDENCE, POLICE SAY

Declare dealer did not know
patrons intended to drink
denatured product

Police said last night they were
informed by the district attorney's
office that the evidence against the
Ellicott street chemical and paint
store proprietor who is alleged to
have sold denatured alcohol to several persons for beverage purposes,
is not sufficient to warrant bringing
the case before the grand jury or for
issuing a warrant.

As a dealer in poisons, the store
proprietor has a right to sell denatured alcohol. He maintained pur-
chasers of the alcohol did not tell
him they intended to drink it.

Sent to Hospital

The store proprietor was questioned when Frank H. Ferguson, 331
Main street, arrested after having
purchased a half a pint of alcohol in
the Ellicott street store, made a
statement saying he intended to drink
the potent mixture, called smoke
because of its cloudy appearance.
Ferguson was later sent to the City
Hospital.

While Ferguson was being questioned, prohibition agents took two
more into custody, after they had
purchased small quantities of the denatured alcohol. They gave their
names as Robert Munn, Swan street
and Thomas Kent, 500 Perry street.
They both made statements to the
police.

The three statements were brought
to the district attorney's office by
police and prohibition agents. Advice that the evidence against the
storekeeper was not sufficient
prompted the announcement that the
case would be dropped.

MARGARET E. WHALEN

MISS WHELAN AGAIN IS QUESTIONED IN MURDER

Authorities make little progress in
locating slayer

Margaret Whelan, reputed friend
of Mrs. Grace Doze, murder victim,
was questioned again last night by
Sheriff Zimmerman in an effort to
identify male friends of the dead woman. The sheriff announced after
the lengthy interrogation that Miss
Whelan would not reveal the names
of any of the men who accompanied
herself and Mrs. Doze on parties. She
was held at the jail again last night.

Chester Doze, husband of the
murder victim, and another woman
who knew her were quizzed by the
sheriff last night, but no information
that might lead to a solution of the
crime was educed.

The automobile mechanic sought
for a day and finally located home
sick, was questioned yesterday afternoon by deputy sheriffs. He satisfied the deputies he knew nothing of
Mrs. Doze's movements the night she
was killed.

Sheriff Zimmerman still is hopeful
that the person who strangled Mrs.
Doze to death and then threw her
body into Ellicott Creek will be ap-
prehended, although he admits the
identity of that person is not known
at the present time.

Fig. 9: Grace's friend held for questioning.

Fig. 10: Margaret refuses to talk.

DOZE QUESTIONED IN WIFE'S DEATH

Important Developments Expected in the Murder Case—Victim Traced to Swimming Class She Attended Tuesday.

County officers Monday afternoon centered their investigation into the murder of Mrs. Grace Doze, whose body was found in Ellicott creek, Wednesday morning, in an effort to determine the movements of the young wife after she left Hutchinson Central High school, where she was known to have been up to 9:30 o'clock Tuesday night.

That she was at the high school and attended a swimming class there was revealed to Sheriff Zimmerman and his investigators Monday, by John K. Wolf, superintendent of swimming in the public schools, and Miss Carlotta C. Boll, swimming instructor at Central-Hutchinson.

Mrs. Doze attended regularly the Tuesday evening swimming classes and was there the night she was last seen alive, according to the statements of Superintendent Wolf and Miss Boll. The names of others who attended the class have been given to Sheriff Zimmerman and they will all be questioned. It was said.

Want to Know Where She Went.

Just now the county investigators desire to learn where Mrs. Doze went after leaving the school. Whether she left alone or in company with some man or woman is not yet known definitely, it is said.

Mrs. Doze had with her a small, black overnight bag in which her swimming equipment was carried. This bag has been found by deputy sheriffs, so it has been announced officially. Sheriff Zimmerman has declined to tell where the bag was found, because of an important bearing the find may have on the ultimate solution of the murder mystery.

Chester G. Doze, husband of the murdered woman, was at the office of District Attorney Guy B. Moore, Monday afternoon ready for an exhaustive examination. It was said, sheriff Zimmerman indicated that he believed important developments would grow out of the questioning of the husband, but declined to indicate the nature of the facts he expected to bring out.

Deputies Sent to Get Him.

Before Doze was taken to the office of District Attorney Moore, Sheriff Zimmerman had expressed concern about the whereabouts of the man and had sent deputies to various parts of the city in search of him.

The sheriff explained this action by a statement that Doze had agreed to report to him Monday morning for examination. As the time passed and Doze failed to appear, Sheriff Zimmerman decided that a search for him was necessary.

Three deputies went to his apartment at 1711 Main street. They found the door unlocked and entered. Doze was not there. They later told the sheriff they searched the apartment and found a hat and brown coat which had belonged to Mrs. Doze. The sheriff ordered them on with the work of locating Doze.

QUIZZED IN WIFE'S DEATH

—Evening News Staff Photo
CHESTER DOZE

... to the Tourist hotel Monday night ... told her mother she was going to Toronto on a visit.

Visited Mother Tuesday.

Sheriff Zimmerman said her daughter did not stay with her Monday night, but came to the house Tuesday morning, and stayed for lunch. She then packed a suitcase and announced she was going to visit a friend, Mrs. Catherine Drago, 911½ College street, Toronto.

Sheriff Zimmerman has established that Mrs. Doze spent Monday night in the Tourist hotel, Michigan and Main streets, where she was registered under the name of Mary Carter, and that she had reserved the same room for use Tuesday night. She was seen in the hotel at 8 o'clock Tuesday evening. The clothes which Mrs. Doze had removed from her mother's house were found in the hotel room Saturday night by a deputy sheriff. The suitcase was missing.

Two Questioned and Freed.

Two men were questioned Saturday night following information supplied by Doze ...

VOELKER GETS 15-YEARS TERM ON RESENTENCE

Previous Conviction of Poisoned Gin Seller Proved in Court So Original Sentence Stands. Goes Back to Auburn to Await Another Appeal.

James C. Voelker, 850 Amherst street, convicted of second degree manslaughter in connection with the death of Mrs. Nellie McCarthy, 47 Wadsworth street, from drinking gin made from wood alcohol last July, was resentenced Monday by Judge F. Bret Thorn in County court to serve 15 years in Auburn prison. According to Walter F. Hofheins, Voelker will immediately be taken back to Auburn.

Before resentencing Voelker to the term he received when convicted last fall, Judge Thorn denied a motion made by Ernest W. McIntyre, attorney for Voelker, for the dismissal of the information laid by the district attorney's office, alleging a former felony conviction against Voelker.

Prove Former Conviction.

It was because an information was not laid at the time Voelker was sentenced last fall that the Appellate division held recently that Voelker had not been shown to be a second offender and should have been given a sentence of only five to ten years.

That sentence was imposed by the appellate division recently. Voelker was then brought to Buffalo, the district attorney's office laid the information alleging a former felony conviction in Federal court and Voelker as the result will go back to Auburn on his original sentence.

Mr. McIntyre announced he will appeal to the appellate division from Judge Thorn's ruling in refusing to dismiss the information.

The information demanded by the Appellate division was filed by the district attorney's office, showing that Voelker September 19, 1923, had pleaded guilty in Federal court to a charge of criminally receiving stolen property. Ernest W. McIntyre, Voelker's counsel, when the case was argued Monday morning before Judge Thorn, held that under the laws of the state of New York the act did not constitute a felony.

Walter F. Hofheins, assistant district attorney, read the federal indictment into the record. The charge was that Voelker and others August 17, 1921, took 162 cases of whisky from a New York Central railroad car. The second charge accused Voelker of possessing the liquor. Voelker pleaded guilty to the second count.

It was Mr. McIntyre's contention that the act of possession is not a felony under the New York law. Mr. Hofheins maintained that Voelker was guilty of criminally receiving stolen property. Both attorneys submitted court decisions and rulings bearing on Voelker's case.

Fig. 11: Chester is questioned.

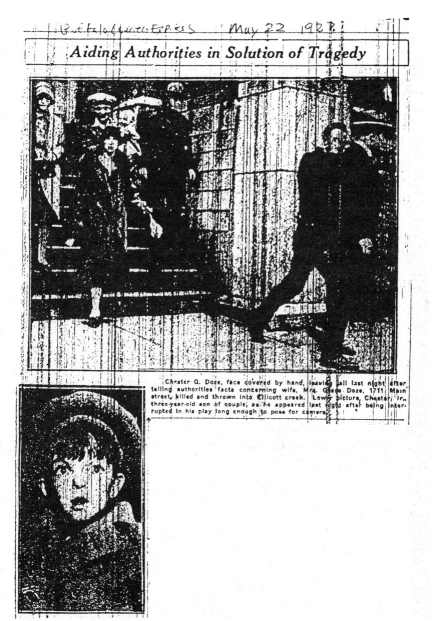

Buffalo Courier Express May 22 1928

Aiding Authorities in Solution of Tragedy

Chester G. Doze, face covered by hand, leaving jail last night after telling authorities facts concerning wife, Mrs. Grace Doze, 1711 Main street, killed and thrown into Ellicott creek. Lower picture, Chester Jr., three-year-old son of couple, as he appeared last night after being interrupted in his play long enough to pose for camera.

Fig. 12: Cliff makes the papers.

elmlawn
MEMORIAL GARDENS
CEMETERY — MAUSOLEUM — CREMATORY — COLUMBARIUM
3939 delaware avenue   kenmore, new york 14217   (716) 876-8131

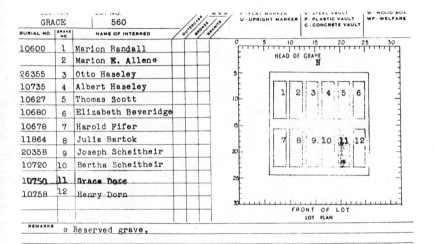

SECTION	LOT NO.		OUTERCISE	BRONZE	GRANITE	M.K.H F.FLAT MARKER S.STEEL VAULT W.WOOD BOX
GRACE	560					U - UPRIGHT MARKER P - PLASTIC VAULT WF - WELFARE C - CONCRETE VAULT

BURIAL NO.	GRAVE NO.	NAME OF INTERRED			
10600	1	Marion Randall			
	2	Marion E. Allen*			
26355	3	Otto Haseley			
10735	4	Albert Haseley			
10627	5	Thomas Scott			
10680	6	Elizabeth Beveridge			
10678	7	Harold Fifer			
11864	8	Julia Bartok			
20358	9	Joseph Scheitheir			
10720	10	Bertha Scheitheir			
10750	11	Grace Dose			
10758	12	Henry Dorn			

REMARKS   * Reserved grave.

elmlawn
MEMORIAL GARDENS
CEMETERY — MAUSOLEUM — CREMATORY — COLUMBARIUM
3939 delaware avenue   kenmore, new york 14217   (716) 876-8131

Fig. 14: Grace's grave site.

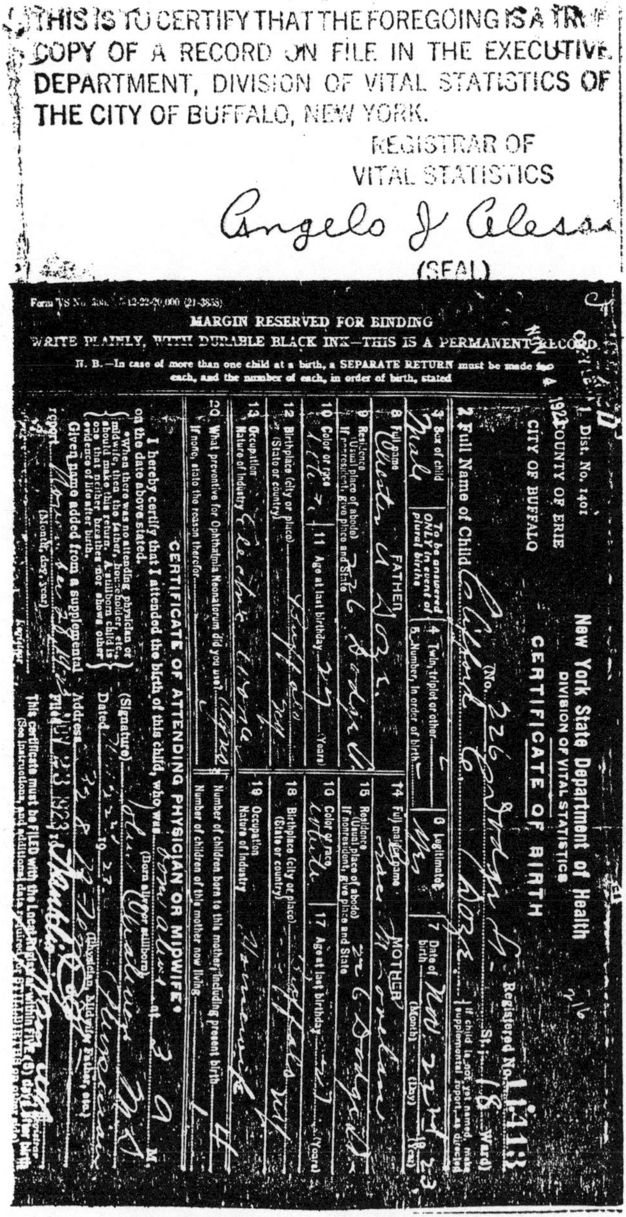

THIS IS TO CERTIFY THAT THE FOREGOING IS A TRUE COPY OF A RECORD ON FILE IN THE EXECUTIVE DEPARTMENT, DIVISION OF VITAL STATISTICS OF THE CITY OF BUFFALO, NEW YORK.

REGISTRAR OF VITAL STATISTICS

Angelo J. Alessa

(SEAL)

MARGIN RESERVED FOR BINDING

WRITE PLAINLY, WITH DURABLE BLACK INK—THIS IS A PERMANENT RECORD

N. B.—In case of more than one child at a birth, a SEPARATE RETURN must be made for each, and the number of each, in order of birth, stated

New York State Department of Health

DIVISION OF VITAL STATISTICS

CERTIFICATE OF BIRTH

1 Dist. No. 1401

COUNTY OF ERIE

CITY OF BUFFALO

2 Full Name of Child Clifford C. Dorze

3 Sex of child Male

8 Full name FATHER

14 Full maiden name MOTHER

CERTIFICATE OF ATTENDING PHYSICIAN OR MIDWIFE

I hereby certify that I attended the birth of this child, who was born alive at 3 A.M. on the date above stated.

Fig. 15: Cliff's birth certificate.

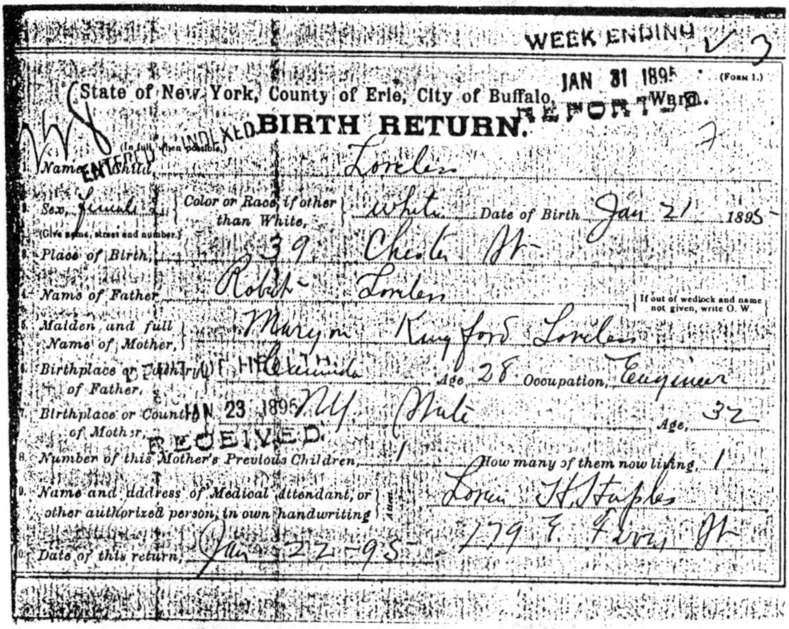

WEEK ENDING

JAN 31 1895 (Form 1.)

State of New York, County of Erie, City of Buffalo, Ward. 7

REPORTED

ENTERED AND INDEXED

BIRTH RETURN.

1. Name of Child, (In full, when possible,) Loveless

2. Sex, female | Color or Race, if other than White, white | Date of Birth Jan 21 1895

3. Place of Birth, (Give name, street and number.) 39 Chester St

4. Name of Father, Robert Loveless | If out of wedlock and name not given, write O. W.

5. Maiden and full Name of Mother, Mary M Kingsford Loveless

6. Birthplace or Country of Father, Canada | Age 28 | Occupation, Engineer

7. Birthplace or Country of Mother, NY State | Age, 32

JAN 23 1896 RECEIVED

8. Number of this Mother's Previous Children, 1 | How many of them now living, 1

9. Name and address of Medical Attendant, or other authorized person, in own handwriting | Loren H Staples 179 E Ferry St

10. Date of this return, Jan 22 - 95

Fig. 16: Grace's birth certificate.

EPILOGUE

On May 16, 1994, the day before the 67th anniversary of her death, Grace Doze made *The Buffalo News* again—a picture of a bouquet of roses placed on the new marker provided for her grave at Elmlawn Cemetery in Tonawanda, New York, by author Bruce Goldberg and *Search for Grace* scriptwriter Alex Ayres.

They hoped she could rest in peace, now.

MORE ON HYPNOSIS

APPENDIX A

How Regression/Progression Hypnotherapy Works

(Some of the material in this chapter and the next appeared in *The Journal of Regression Therapy*, Volume VII, Number 1, December 1993, pp. 89–93, in my article titled "Quantum Physics and Its Application to Past-Life Regression and Future-Life Progression Hypnotherapy." It is presented here with permission from the publisher.)

One of the most misconstrued words in the English language is "Hypnosis." The word is taken from the Greek "hypnos" and literally means sleep. Hypnosis, however, occurs on the natural daydream level that we all experience from three to four hours daily. It is an alpha brain-wave level, as measured by the electroencephalograph (EEG). Without the restorative effects of the alpha level, we would die of stroke or heart attack due to inability to deal with stress.

Hypnosis is thus a natural state, which everyone has logged for 1100 to 1500 hours of every year of his life. Since everyone goes through self-hypnosis daily, everyone, theoretically, can be hypnotized. In fact, five percent of the population is refractive, meaning they block any attempt of a therapist to guide them into self-hypnosis. The patient has so much control over this state that he or she may block it or terminate the trance at any time. For a more detailed explanation of hypnosis, I refer you to Chapter Two of my book, *Past Lives–Future Lives*.

Most therapists assume that hypnosis must deal with visual imagery and behavior modification and must be administered at a fairly deep level to be effective. With all due respect to my colleagues, this simply is not true. First of all, the depth of trance is irrelevant. Any "cleansing" regression and progression technique can be done at light, medium, or deep trance levels. Also, visual imagery is not necessary or even desirable when "cleansing" is performed. Lastly, this technique is *not* behavior modification. What I generally achieve with my patients is an energy cleansing or a raising of the vibrational rate of their alpha brain wave (subconscious mind).

This alpha level produces electromagnetic radiation which is equivalent to a television or radio signal. Unfortunately, the undeveloped soul (or spirit or subconscious mind—the terms are interchangeable) operates in our current body at a relatively low frequency of vibrational rate. Chapters 3, 5, 24, and 25 in *Past Lives–Future Lives*, explain this concept in greater detail. Since the purpose of karma, and thus the process of reincarnation, is to purify the soul, it must raise this frequency somehow.

As we go through each life we face challenges, sometimes referred to as karmic tests. If we pass the test, our frequency is raised. However, if we fail a challenge, a lowered frequency vibrational rate results. Cleansing is the process through which the hypnotherapist introduces the patient's subconscious mind to its superconscious or higher self. This superconscious mind level is perfect, and thus accessing or tapping into this level results in a raising of the energy level of the patient's subconscious mind. Therapy is accomplished through tapping into this superconscious mind and viewing the akashic records or conversing with one's masters and guides.

As I stated in *Past Lives–Future Lives* (167-168):

> Since basically all of my patients present themselves with an array of self-defeating sequences (SDS), it is critical to remove these blocks before any long-lasting progress can be achieved.
>
> Good examples of self-defeating sequences are procrastination, lateness, compulsive spending, alcoholism, overeating, impatience, etc. One tends to create difficulties in one's life (and lives) which prevent one from achieving desired goals, whether personal or professional. The self-image (how we perceive ourselves, not how others perceive us) is lowered.
>
> The first step in hypnotherapy is to improve this self-image. If you build a house on quicksand, it won't be around to benefit by appreciation. I have already discussed the use of cassette tapes personally recorded by myself for my patients to help establish a sound and strong psychological foundation from which patients can more fully understand their karmic purpose and make strides toward fulfilling their karma.

Most of a patient's therapy will take effect during the dream level at night. Recent medical research establishes that we enter REM (rapid eye movement), a characteristic of the dream state, for three hours each night. Since our defense mechanisms (will-power or analytical mind) cannot function once we enter the sleep cycle, this is a most efficient cleansing opportunity.

During this dream state, the emotional cleansing necessary for our survival occurs. But deeper energy cleansing is not part of this survival function. It will not occur unless we are trained for it. If we are properly trained, we will use approximately one hour of the REM cycle to cleanse our alpha level. Since each minute in hypnosis is equivalent to three to four earth minutes, three to four hours of therapeutic energy cleansing is actually experienced by the patient. It is no wonder that this therapy is so short, successful and popular. The patient is trained in a relatively few sessions to be totally independent of the therapist and to attain any goal that is humanly possible. The patient uses superconscious mind tapes to assist in this goal.

There are three levels of manifestation of an issue. First, there is the physical level. Using depression as an example, the associated lack of energy and malaise are examples of the physical level. Next is the emotional level. In this example, unexplained crying would be a symptom of this level. The last and most important level is the energy level. This level is the actual frequency vibrational rate of the patient's alpha level or subconscious mind. In other words, this is the level of spiritual growth or karmic status of the individual.

The energy level controls the emotional level which in turn influences the physical level. Thus, the only level I am concerned with when I conduct a hypnotherapy session is the energy level. Once we raise the patient's frequency vibrational rate to a new threshold—a major breakthrough—this new level or rate is established and irreversible. The patient may plateau for a while, but this new rate cannot be lowered. Thus, the emotional and physical symptoms as well as the causes are resolved by treating the ultimate cause, which is the patient's energy level or frequency vibrational rate.

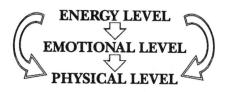

You will note that the arrows always flow down from the energy level to the physical but not in reverse; also observe that the energy level can change the physical level directly without having to use the emotional level as an intermediary. An example of this latter phenomenon would be the removal of psychosomatic pain or a headache.

Because each level supports an immune system, a superconscious mind tap can result in the remission of a cancer tumor. This is explained in detail in my 1985 article entitled "The Treatment of Cancer Through Hypnosis." Raising energy levels can also increase the emotional level's immune system so that a patient can be exposed to certain recurring influences or circumstances without reverting to old emotional behavior patterns such as grief, anxiety, depression, etc. In my Woodland Hills, California, office, I see many patients who suffer from bereavement over the death of a young child or a spouse; this technique allows me to quickly guide the patient into resolving this issue. This approach can also work with just about any issue that is reversible.

How does past-life regression, age progression, or future-life progression fit into this approach? The answer is simple. These techniques are used as stepping stones to reach the superconscious mind and to satisfy the patient's curiosity. These techniques taken together account for approximately five percent of the therapy. Ninety-five percent of any therapeutic result will come from cleansing at the superconscious level. This cleansing will also greatly reduce the time and number of sessions required to train patients to resolve their conflicts and maximize their potential.

Since this is not cognitive or analytical therapy, I am not particularly interested in the intellectual "cause" of the issue. In this type of therapy, process is everything. The whys are not important. All the patient has to do is be motivated to attain a goal, have that goal be possible to attain, and trust the therapist he works with. As long as these three conditions are met, any goal is achievable.

There is a growing need in all fields of psychotherapy today for more effective methods of treatment. Successful therapy should facilitate the patient's gaining increased mastery over himself so he can learn to cope with and overcome his problems. The majority of psychotherapy methods are either too limited in their applications, too lengthy, or too costly. The recovery rate, judged by empirical observations, can be meaningful only if it exceeds the sixty-five percent spontaneous cure rate (the placebo effect.)

Quantum physics can explain regression and progression by a series of equations illustrating a space-time continuum in which all time is simultaneous. According to Wolf (1981), there is something other than space-time, something nonphysical, not measurable, and beyond all laws of physics, which is pure consciousness. It is our alpha brain wave level which is, of course, what we deal with in hypnotherapy.

The new physics tells us that we influence our futures (and pasts) directly with thought. This is not will power but awareness; what we visualize is what we see. There is no physical world without our thoughts about it. If we are "hung up" on the past, we will choose to see the future as we saw the past, and the SDS will repeat themselves. If we alter our perception of the present via hypnotic programming (Goldberg, 1985), then our altered view will change the future.

The future is not predestined; it is mutable. With positive programming in the here and now, supplemented by the patient's perception and cleansing away of energy blocks incurred in past and future lifetimes, one can help place the patient on a far more positive and productive path (Goldberg, 1988). One of the problems psychotherapists have with this field is that they label any "voices" a patient hears (as will occasionally happen with superconscious mind taps) as pathologic (schizophrenics, for example, hear voices on a regular basis), and incorrectly equate these voices with auditory hallucinations.

The growing field of transpersonal psychology (Code 395 of the American Psychology Association's Major Field Division) strongly supports this approach. Terms such as superconscious (Assagioli) are being used to suggest different levels of being within the individual. According to Assagioli (1965, p. 113), "Transpersonal will is an expression of the Transpersonal Self and operates from the subconscious levels of the psyche. It is its action which is felt by the personal self."

The interplay of these intrapsychic levels may express itself as the experience of an inner voice. This experience should not be classified as pathological, but rather be considered as a striving toward fulfillment of various aspects of the individual. According to Assagioli, superconscious energies work with the individual according to the levels at which he/she can receive and integrate these energies. The positive outcome of such an experience is that the individual can be directed to the next steps necessary for fuller integration.

Hypnotherapy is classified as Code 07.01.05, and parapsychology as Code 270 on the American Psychological Association's APA field system. The American Association for the Advancement of Science in Washington, D.C., formally accepted parapsychology into its family of sciences in 1969. Most people are unfamiliar with the enormous credibility of this "unconventional" field. Also, since past-life regression/progression hypnotherapy is based on the principles of quantum physics (see Chapter 3 of *Past-Lives–Future Lives*), that makes this field the only one accepted by the APA that is based on a hard science.

What you know depends on the state of consciousness you are in. Research into altered states of consciousness has shown us that some kinds of human knowledge are state specific. If you aren't in a certain state of consciousness, certain things cannot be known (Wolf, 1981).

It is necessary to differentiate between the terms "fate" and "destiny." Fate corresponds approximately with our concept of what has been decreed, or our past action (karma). We feel ourselves to be victims of fate, caught in its web, or net. Destiny, on the other hand, which corresponds loosely with the Indian notion of dharma, is future oriented, free and flexible; it is our purpose or destination, what we choose to be and do, our prime intention in this life. We fulfill our destiny by exercising our free will. Superconscious mind taps and cleansing allow patients to maximize their free will and thus fulfill their destiny.

Numerous theorists have produced "maps" of consciousness, attempting to describe various characteristics and types of consciousness. Although few of these theorists use terminology in the same way, they usually recognize a general ordering of states of consciousness according to their "distance" from the ordinary waking state of consciousness. Transpersonal refers to experience in which one leaves or transcends normal consciousness for another and presumably nonrational (though not irrational) state of consciousness which is "higher" and may be identified with the Divine in some cases.

In the teachings of yoga, the transpersonal stage is seen as intermediate, rather than the final goal in the development of consciousness. Transcendent Consciousness is the final goal of meditation. The basic process of meditation consists of letting go of all limiting identifications, whether worldly or fantastic, earthly or heavenly, in order to reach that Supreme Consciousness which is unfettered. In this way, meditation leads one beyond the unconscious to that Supreme Awareness which is the fulfillment of human life.

"Transpersonal psychology" is concerned with such areas as unitive consciousness and transcendental phenomena, while "parapsychology" is the scientific study of the extrasensory motor behavior of organisms. Psi phenomena may occur in certain of the altered conscious states which are of special interest to many transpersonal psychologists. Examples would include dreams, meditation, out-of-body experiences, psychedelic states, near-death encounters, and past/future-life experiences. Transpersonal experience usually occurs without ostensible psi phenomena.

One current development is an interest in life after death, the topic parapsychologists call "the survival question." Another is the increased interest in "psychic healing" and the accelerating research in this area. Both fields are matters of practical concern of life and death. If a transpersonal experience is defined as one in which an individual transcends his usual ego boundaries as well as the dimensions of time and space, then there can be little doubt that individuals who survive a near-death experience have entered a transpersonal state of consciousness.

Wilber (1979) breaks down awareness into seven levels:

1. The gross realm: the physical body and all lower levels of consciousness, including the psychoanalytic ego and simple sensations and perceptions.

2. The astral realm: out-of-the-body experiences and certain occult knowledge.

3. The psychic realm: psi phenomena such as ESP, clairvoyance, and precognition.

4.   The subtle realm: higher symbolic visions, light, higher presences, and intense but soothing vibrations and bliss.

5.   The lower causal realm: beginning of true transcendence and the undermining of subject-object dualism.

6.   The higher causal realm: transcendence of all manifest realms.

7.   The ultimate: absolute identity with the Many and the One.

Parapsychology can provide a basic and fundamental underpinning to transpersonal psychology, in the same way that physics is a basic science underlying engineering. We all know, of course, that parapsychology has not been generally accepted among orthodox scientists, but that is an emotional matter, not a scientific one, and the situation is changing in positive ways.

TRANSPERSONAL PSYCHOTHERAPY (Bugental, 1978)

Transpersonal psychotherapy may be conceived as an open-ended endeavor to facilitate human growth and expand awareness beyond the limits implied by most traditional Western models of mental health. However, in the process of enlarging one's felt sense of identity to include transpersonal dimensions of being, the therapist may employ traditional therapeutic techniques as well as hypnosis and other awareness exercises derived from Eastern consciousness disciplines.

Since transpersonal psychotherapy is concerned with the attainment of levels of psychological health which surpass what is commonly accepted as normal, it is useful to define some goals of therapy. One goal is to develop the capacity for taking responsibility for oneself in the world and in one's relationships. It may also be assumed that the healthy person is capable of experiencing a full range of emotions while remaining relatively detached from the personal melodrama. Another goal is to enable each person to meet physical, emotional, mental, and spiritual needs appropriately, in accordance with individual preferences and predisposition. Hence, no one path can be expected to be appropriate for everyone. In transpersonal psychotherapy, impulses toward spiritual growth are considered basic to full humanness. It is assumed that in addition to basic survival needs for food, shelter and relationship, higher need for self-realization must be met for full functioning at optimum levels of health.

From a transpersonal viewpoint, every patient is seen as having the capacity for self-healing. In other words, the therapist does not cure an ailment for a patient, but enables a patient to tap inner resources and allow the natural healing or growth process to occur. Furthermore, the human organism is seen as seeking to enhance and surpass itself in the process of self-actualization. This implies that it has potential for bringing into being those qualities and capacities that may be latent or underdeveloped within the person experiencing conflict or stress. Beyond this is the possibility of self-transcendence or transpersonal realization in which the separate and isolated ego may be experienced as illusory, while the underlying oneness of existence is experienced as real.

In transpersonal psychotherapy patients are given the opportunity to experience transcendence and awakening. One psychiatrist, after becoming personally involved in a spiritual practice, noticed that his patients, for the first time in twenty years, began to voice their spiritual concerns, even though he did not mention his interest.

This transpersonal world view is supported by both modern (quantum) physics and Eastern mysticism, which describes the universe as a dynamic, intricate web of relationships in continuous change. As one becomes aware of the transpersonal dimension of being, values and behavior tend to change. Problems that remain insoluble at the ego level may now be transcended. Once a person has awakened to the transpersonal dimensions of existence, life itself may be held in a different perspective. A new sense of meaning may well be the content derived from the newly experienced transpersonal self as context. Although a transcendent experience per se is not necessarily required for the development of this awareness, it frequently seems to accelerate the process of disidentification and awakening. Paradoxically, the experience of disidentification and transcendence and the awakening to the transpersonal self also tends to be accompanied by a sense of personal freedom and a renewed sense of inner directedness and responsibility.

The spectrum of Consciousness is a pluridimensional approach to man's identity. Man's innermost consciousness is identical to the absolute and ultimate reality of the universe, known variously as Brahman, Tao, Dharmakaya, Allah, the godhead, to name but a few, and which, for the sake of convenience, I will simply call Mind. According to this universal tradition, Mind is what there is and all there is; spaceless and therefore infinite; timeless and therefore eternal, outside of which nothing exists. The superconscious mind tap is one way to reach this Mind.

Some individuals diagnosed as schizophrenic may indeed be psychologically lost in some of the lower energy levels or parallel universes for want of an adequate guide. But there remains an essential difference between various transpersonal mystical experiences, such as peak experiences, and schizophrenia. Although the schizophrenic may strongly experience a partial fusion of opposites, such as self and other, past and future, inside and outside, this fusion generally produces feelings of pervasive disorientation and confusion, while in the mystic, it produces feelings of profound simplicity and clarity. Mysticism is fusion without confusion; schizophrenia is fusion with confusion.

The collapse of the dualism between subject and object is simultaneously the collapse of the dualism between past and future, life and death, so that one awakens as if from a dream to the spaceless and timeless world of cosmic consciousness. Transpersonal psychotherapy addresses these issues.

I would like to end this section with some advice to psychotherapists who have decided to utilize transpersonal approaches in their practice. Any label you place on a patient is entrapping because labels are limiting; they are finite; they have suffering connected with them. And part of the work of consciousness is to redefine your own being, your own nature, to the point where you are, and then there's the psychiatrist-ness, and there's womanness, and there's personality-ness, and there's opportunity-ness, and so on; these are more like phenomenal rings around your essence rather than who you are. As long as you think you're somebody who's doing something, you are caught in some kind of suffering.

Freud saw the psychosexual stages of development as real, and Adler saw power as real, and Jung saw archetypes as real; and they are all relatively real, like Newtonian physics is relatively real, and in the same way, Einsteinian physics is relatively real. But the existence of Einsteinian physics made us all aware of how Newtonian physics was only relatively real, while previously we treated it as absolute. Once you live in a universe where you experience even your living and dying as relative rather than in absolute terms, it's all free to change. There's nowhere you have to go to work on yourself other than where you are at this moment, and everything that's happening to you is part of your work on yourself. All you do is root yourself deeper in what it is that it is about. What is transformation? What does Christ mean when he says, "Die and be born again"? What are the Tzaddiks talking about in the Hassidic tradition? What is Buddha talking about? What is Rama Krishna saying, or the Christina mystics, the Sufi saint Rumi, and people like this? If you read the writings of these beings, and you experience what it is they are referring to, then you begin to work with your daily life in order to convert it to just being a light, being a beacon. You're really nothing, but the more nothing you are, the more the light comes through. More and more I think I am less and less. I'm putting myself down; I'm right here, but I'm not busy thinking about who I am. There's much less self-consciousness in life.

APPENDIX B

The Space-Time Continuum

In presenting some of the scientific theories from quantum physics, I hope to suggest some ways in which quantum physics supports regression and progression therapy. In order to fully understand the concept of regressing into previous lives and progressing into future lifetimes, in fact, we must discuss quantum physics. Quantum physics and quantum mechanics aren't mysterious, just initially a little hard to understand. Without getting involved with complicated mathematics, I would like to present this hard-science foundation to our work with hypnotherapy.

The Washington Post on April 21, 1985, page 101, ran an article by Eugene F. Mallove on this concept. In it Einstein's theory of relativity was discussed. "There is no universal 'now,' no universal 'past' and no universal 'future.'" The work of physicist Richard Feynman, in which he postulated that a positron (a positively charged electron) was nothing more than an electron moving backward in time, was described. Since these particles move faster than the speed of light, they can move backward or forward in time (Wolf, 1981).

When I began to use progression hypnotherapy in 1977, I noted that some dreams seemed to be important sneak previews of future events, both in this life (age progression) and in future lifetimes (future-life progression).

Several theories of precognition have been advanced. Most are abstruse, some ingenious, none adequate. Basically, these theories fall into two categories. The first looks on the future as an already existent reality, one that exists as fully and objectively as the present does. The future is not a potentiality but an actuality. The second postulates a "plastic" or provisional future which exists now in somewhat the same way that a human being exists the instant the sperm meets the ovum. A lot can happen to a fetus between conception and birth, and possibly the same sort of incident—abortion, miscarriage, premature delivery—can occur to an event gestating in the "womb of time."

Many dreams seem to contain fragments of futuristic material, just as they contain fragments from the past. In sleep, the mind appears to wander freely back and forth over the "equator," an imaginary line between the present and the future. At the deepest level of consciousness, there is no sense of the flow of time, only an "eternal now" in which all events coexist. The theory of a plastic future rejects the notion that the future already exists. It says that tomorrow is real only in potentiality. The future is capable of taking many possible final forms. Only when it congeals into the present does it really exist as an actuality.

An interesting sidelight to the idea that we dream the future as well as the past is that it offers an explanation for what is the most common of all psychic experiences, *deja vu*. This is the strange sensation one sometimes experiences when encountering a new scene or situation that nevertheless seems oddly familiar. Conventional psychology tends to label such experiences as paramnesia, a defect of memory in which the person's sense of before and after gets confused. However, among those who have carefully studied deja vu, even psychologists who have no sympathy for the supernormal, the phenomenon cannot be so easily dismissed.

Deja vu may stem from precognitive dreams. If events that were foredreamed actually take place, we have the vague feeling that it has all happened to us before. However, we do not remember that we dreamed it. Studies have revealed that almost everyone dreams approximately three hours every night, but only a few of the dreams are remembered on awakening. A variation on the usual deja vu theme is double deja vu, when two people share the experience. I have discussed these concepts more thoroughly in Chapter 14 of *Past Lives–Future Lives*.

Time and space are interrelated. Since Einstein, this concept is not news to anyone, but it is because of this space-time continuum that we can peer backward in time as we peer outward in space. The astronomer gazing through his telescope is traversing years as well as miles.

Parallel Universes

Wolf (1988) discusses the concept of parallel universes, presenting many ideas that may be relevant to work with past-life regression and future-life progression. He points out that there are parallel universes in which exist human beings who may be exact duplicates of ourselves, and they may be connected to us through mechanisms available to us only through quantum physics. In these universes different choices are being made at the same time you and I make our choices. The outcomes are different and thus the worlds are similar but still different. An indefinite number of futures and pasts can communicate with our present.

Wolf also states that it is within a black hole that the theory of relativity and parallel universes meet. A black hole represents a place in space in which time and space appear to fold over on top of each other. The gravitational field created is theorized to be so intense that nothing, not even light, can escape. He points out that it is possible to perceive and select another path (future frequency) to experience. Wolf postulates that delusions, alien abductions and "miracles" might be explained by the perception ("peeking in") of a parallel universe.

A picture is worth a thousand words. Wolf and Toben (1982) use Everett's metaphor of a flipped coin to illustrate the concept of parallel universes:

> For example, when you flip a coin in the air, it lands on the ground with heads or tails showing, never both sides at the same time. But the coin's quantum wave always gives equal probability of heads or tails showing. How can the wave represent reality? Everett and his followers came up with the answer that for each possibility there exists a parallel universe where the event actually occurs. Thus, in one universe the coin lands heads and in another it lands tails. And even more surprising, you are in both universes observing the coin's fate. You exist in each world. Yet each world is essentially unknown to the other (p.130).

Hugh Everett was a graduate student in quantum physics at Princeton University who, in 1957, discovered the concept of parallel universes and used this concept as the basis of his dissertation for his doctorate. Wolf and Toben state that Everett's work showed that there are an infinite number of parallel universes.

Even though there are, theoretically, an infinite number of parallel universes (frequencies), my experience since 1977 with over 5,000 progressions suggests that for human beings there are five main frequencies. That is, there is an infinite number of subfrequencies, but they seem to fall into five main categories and groups. Thus, you may have a million variations of frequency number one, but the basic framework is similar. Frequencies numbered two through five will have very different frameworks or basic events, but within each of these groups (frequencies), the framework is similar. Your five frequencies may be quite different from mine, depending on the frequency vibrational rate (level of spiritual growth) of your subconscious mind (soul). Through progression hypnotherapy you can lay out these five paths, select the best one and be programmed for your most attractive future.

In Chapter 22 of *Past Lives–Future Lives*, I described the case of a man who progressed to the year 2088, experienced a nervous breakdown, and caused a melt-down of a nuclear research facility in Tulsa, Oklahoma. This patient was progressed to the other four frequencies and chose a different frequency to be programmed to; he "switched tracks." On this frequency he was psychologically stable and this catastrophe was averted.

In conclusion, by having patients perceive their future options in this life as well as in future lifetimes, they are empowered to be in control of their own destiny by selecting and being programmed to their ideal frequencies. I personally find this most rewarding. The fact that each and every one of my patients can control his own destiny is indeed fulfilling.

APPENDIX C

Self-Hypnosis And Seeking Hypnotherapy

It can be frustrating to read a book such as this and not be able to identify experientially with the natural state of hypnosis. No matter how well it is explained, a naive reader often simply cannot identify with the process. (A complete exposition of hypnosis is offered in Chapter Two of *Past Lives–Future Lives*.) I therefore include the following simple explanation and exercise that I developed in my early years in private practice.

Hypnosis is a subject of rich interest to nearly everyone. The fascination that it holds is its promise to open to a person a world of rich treasure and self-improvement as if by magic. And nearly everyone who is human finds at some time he has a desire or need to improve himself. Hypnosis seems to provide an answer. After all, we've all seen how hypnotists have the power to make people do things, haven't we? We use the adjective "hypnotic" interchangeably with "compelling."

But the hypnotist, in fact, has no power and never did, just skill. The hypnotists who come to mind were professional entertainers who deliberately tried to give the false impression that they had a "remarkable power" over the subject and could force him to do things. The actual power behind hypnosis lies within the subject and his mind. Charged and unleashed, he is free to release all his mental creative power and bring it to bear with amazing results. The capacity of the human mind to solve and create is remarkable. Self-hypnosis and hypnotic techniques are a way to successfully reach and put to use more of one's own mind.

Genuine and legitimate improvements in one's self are never simple and easy. They require persistence and determination to accomplish; without these, failure will follow.

Hypnosis is pleasant. It is a state of deep concentration. Your **conscious** mind is relatively weak. It vacillates continuously and will create an endless round of excuses as to why you should not bother with what you are trying to accomplish. It lacks the kind of stabilizing force that the **subconscious** possesses.

The **subconscious** mind can best be influenced when one is in a passive or relaxed state, such as in hypnosis. This restful quieting of the mind acts to cleanse it, opening it to pure and more elevated thoughts. Hypnosis will build both mental vigor and enthusiasm because it removes all the negative fears and thoughts that act as roadblocks to energy, inspiration and accomplishment. You must turn your wishes, ideas or hopes into reality, or they remain meaningless to you. The subconscious is the best place to start the undertaking.

I suggest, therefore, that two periods a day be put aside for the purpose of training your subconscious mind. The periods need be only ten minutes. The best time is very early in the morning shortly after awakening. Another period can be at your convenience during the day, except before bedtime, unless you are having difficulty in falling asleep.

Stage 1: Find a quiet room and close the door to shut out distracting sounds. Lie down on a bed or couch and relax as best you can for about two to five minutes. Both the mind and body will tend to relax as you lay inert, and this passive state will open a door to the subconscious mind. As you lie quietly, close your eyes and think of a warm, relaxing feeling.

A. Focus all your attention on the muscles in the toes of both your feet. Imagine this warm, relaxing feeling spreading and surrounding the muscles of the toes, moving to the backs of both feet and to the heels and ankles. Now imagine this warm feeling moving up the calf muscles of both legs to the kneecap and into the thigh muscles, meeting at the hip bone.

B. The warm, relaxing feeling is moving up the backbone to the middle of the back, surrounding the shoulder blades and moving into the back of the neck.

C. The warm, relaxing feeling is now moving into the fingers of both hands, just like it did with the toes. This feeling now spreads into the backs of both hands, palms, wrists, forearms, elbows, shoulders and neck, relaxing each and every muscle along its path.

D. This warm, relaxing feeling moves into the back of the head, scalp and all the way to the

forehead. Now, the facial muscles are relaxed; the eyes, which are closed; the
bridge of the nose, the mouth, the chin,
ear lobes and neck. Now each and every
muscle in the entire body is completely relaxed.

When you develop this generalized relaxed feeling throughout your body with an accompanying heaviness in your arms or
legs, you have finally reached a light state of hypnosis. Continue
with the exercise for several days, then progress to the second
stage. The instructions should become a part of the mental
dialogue that you will be thinking to yourself. Read it over two
or three times and commit the general idea to memory, rather
than trying to remember it word for word.

Stage 2: To go deeper into hypnosis is the
next concern. This can be accomplished in a
number of ways. One of the more common is to
imagine a very pleasant and soothing scene, such
as a green valley that you are looking down into
from a mountain top, watching a lazy brook me-
ander, relaxing you more and more as you watch
its slow movements. Another way is to imagine
yourself descending a flight of stairs very slowly
while thinking to yourself as you wind down the
ancient stone stairwell that you are going deeper
and deeper and deeper with each step. The following is an example of a hypnotist deepening the
hypnotic trance state:

"I want you to imagine that you are standing
on the fifth floor of a large department store . . .
and that you are just stepping into the elevator to
descend to street level. And as you go down, and
as the elevator door opens and closes as you arrive

at each floor . . . you will become more and more deeply relaxed . . . and your sleep will become deeper and deeper.

The doors are closing now . . . and you are beginning to sink slowly downwards. The elevator stops at the fourth floor . . . several people get out . . . two more get in . . . the doors close again . . . and already you are becoming more and more deeply relaxed . . . more and more deeply asleep.

And as you sink to the third floor . . . and stop, while the doors open and close again . . . you are relaxing more and more . . . and your sleep is becoming deeper and deeper.

You slowly sink down to the second floor . . one or two people get out and several get in . . and as they do so . . . you are feeling much more deeply relaxed . . . much more deeply asleep.

Down once again to the first floor . . . the doors open and close . . . but nobody gets out or in. Already you have become still more deeply relaxed . . . and you sleep still deeper and deeper. Deeper and deeper asleep . . . deeper and deeper asleep.

Down further and further . . . until the elevator stops at last at street level. The doors open . . . and everybody gets out.

But you do not get out.

You decide to go still deeper . . . and descend to the basement.

The elevator doors close again . . . and down you go . . . down and down . . . deeper and deeper . . . and as you arrive at the basement . . . you are feeling twice as deeply and comfortably relaxed . . . twice as deeply asleep."

As you develop skill with your own mind, you will be able to go under much more quickly, and even surroundings that used to be too distracting for you to handle will now become tolerable for practicing self-hypnosis.

SEEKING HYPNOTHERAPY

Many people contact my Los Angeles office with questions and requests for referrals. Since I cannot refer a patient to a therapist without knowing quite a lot about the therapist's training and experience in this field, I would like to include some general suggestions that first appeared in *Past Lives–Future Lives* (274):

Although I know of no case in which hypnosis has ever harmed anyone, I highly recommend that you seek out a qualified hypnotherapist. The term hypnotherapist should only be used by someone with a doctorate in the health sciences. It may be a D.D.S. (such as myself), it may be a Ph.D. (such as a psychologist), or an M.D. (a physician), or other health professional.

The term hypnotist refers to those without professional background other than their training in hypnosis, which may have been as little as four days. I recommend a doctor because doctors subscribe to strong ethical codes which a lay hypnotist may or may not adhere to. Second, our background includes much training in psychology and other behavioral sciences.

The second quality I would look for in a hypnotherapist is a very extensive background in the field of parapsychology. He or she should be knowledgeable about all aspects of karma and be able to answer your questions and offer the appropriate guidance.

The third quality to look for is experience. The therapist should have done regressions or progressions many, many times before. He should also be experienced in shielding (white-light protection) techniques, which should precede any regression or progression.

Fourth, trust your instinct about the therapist. If the therapist is qualified but you don't like or trust him or her, leave immediately. Not only will you not succeed with this particular therapist, but you might just be susceptible to his or her negative karma.

Since 1958, the American Medical Association has formally accepted hypnosis as a reputable clinical aid. The British Medical Association accepted hypnosis in 1955. No longer are hypnotherapists thought of as charlatans or stage entertainers. When I first began practicing hypnotherapy, patients would seek my services as a last resort, usually after traditional medicine and psychotherapy had failed. Today, I'm more often approached initially, before other traditional forms of therapy are considered. Of course, I refer my patients to physicians to rule out possible physiological causes of their complaints. When the physical causes of illness are eliminated, I begin my therapy. Any therapist you consider should take this clinical approach.

Always use your common sense when undergoing past-life regression hypnotherapy. Please don't attach any significance to what a psychic or "past-life reader" tells you about your past lives. Anyone can say that you were Queen Nefertiti, but in reality, in conducting over 30,000 past-life regressions since 1974, I have never regressed anyone to the life of an historical figure.

The only credibility I would place on such information would be if it came directly from the patient and was conducted by a credible hypnotherapist. There is no such thing as a degree in hypnosis, least of all a doctorate. Credible therapists have degrees in medicine, dentistry, psychology, social work, etc. Make sure the person you are considering seeing has degrees (a minimum degree should be a Master's Degree) from an accredited university. There are plenty of diploma mills around that offer phony Ph.D.'s and theology degrees to anyone with the right amount of money. Please do yourself and the rest of the universe a favor by keeping away from these charlatans. If your prospective therapist has a Doctor of Divinity degree (D.D.), it should be from an accredited seminary or other university. Pastoral counseling is perfectly acceptable as long as the credentials are in order.

I highly recommend *Past Lives–Future Lives* for a more detailed explanation of hypnosis and its clinical application. Many different types of problems are discussed therein, with dynamic case histories. Those of you interested in further information on this technique will find this an informative source.

I would like to end this section with a list of some of the many benefits that can be attained through hypnotherapy:

1. Increased relaxation and the elimination of tension.

2. Increased and focused concentration.

3. Improved memory ("hypernesia").

4. Improved reflexes.

5. Increased self-confidence.

6. Pain control.

7. Improved sex life.

8. Increased organization and efficiency.

9. Increased motivation.

10. Improved interpersonal relationships.

11. Slowing down the aging process.

12. Harmony of the mind, body, and spirit.

13.   Elimination of habits, phobias, and other negative tendencies.

14.   Improved psychic awareness—ESP, meditation, astral projection (out-of-body experience), telepathy.

15.   Elimination of the fear of death by viewing one's past and future lives.

———. 1990. "The Clinical Use of Hypnotic Regression and ...

BIBLIOGRAPHY

Assagioli, R. 1986. *Self-Realization and Psychological Disturbances.* Revision 8(2), 21-31.

Bugental, J. 1978. *Psychotherapy and Process: The Fundamentals of an Existential Humanistic Approach.* Reading, Mass.: Addison-Wesley.

Fisher, Joe. 1984. *The Case for Reincarnation.* New York: Bantam Books.

Goldberg, Bruce. 1993. "Quantum Physics and Its Application to Past-Life Regression and Future-Life Progression Hypnotherapy." *Journal of Regression Therapy,* v. 7-1, 89-93.

———. 1990. "The Clinical Use of Hypnotic Regression and Progression in Hypnotherapy." *Psychology–A Journal of Human Behavior,* v. 27-1, 43-48.

———. 1990. "Your Problem May Come from Your Future: A Case Study. *Journal of Regression Therapy,* v. 4-2, 21-29.

———. 1988. *Past Lives–Future Lives.* New York: Ballantine Books.

———. 1987. "Hypnotherapy: A Combined Approach Using Psychotherapy and Behavior Modification." *Psychology–A Journal of Human Behavior, v.* 24-3, 37-40.

———. 1985. "The Treatment of Cancer Through Hypnosis." *Psychology–A Journal of Human Behavior, v.* 3-4, 36-39.

———. 1985. "Hypnosis and the Immune Response." *International Journal of Psychosomatics, v.* 3-3, 24-26.

———. 1984. "Treating Dental Phobias Through Past-Life Therapy: A Case Report." *Journal of the Maryland State Dental Association, v.* 27-3, 137-139.

Jarocinski, Stefan. 1965. *Polish Music.* Warsaw: Polish Scientific Publishers.

Monroe, Robert A. 1971. *Journeys Out of the Body.* New York: Doubleday.

Moody, Raymond A. 1975. *Life After Life.* New York: Bantam Books.

Ostrander, Sheila and Schroeder, Lynn. 1970. *Psychic Discoveries Behind the Iron Curtain.* New York: Bantam Books.

Targ, Russell and Harvy, Keith. 1984. *The Mind Race.* New York: Villard Books.

Ten Dam, Hans, 1990. *Exploring Reincarnation.* London: Arkana Books.

Wells, H.B. 1971. *The Outline of History.* New York: Doubleday & Co., Inc.

Wilber, K.A. 1979. "Developmental View of Consciousness." *Journal of Transpersonal Psychology, v.* 11-1, 1-21.

Wolf, Fred A. 1981. *Taking the Quantum Leap.* New York: Harper & Row.

———, and Toben, Bob. 1982. *Space-Time and Beyond.* New York: Bantam Books.

———. 1988. *Parallel Universes: The Search for Other Worlds.* New York: Simon & Schuster.

ABOUT THE AUTHOR

Dr. Bruce Goldberg graduated from Southern Connecticut State College in June, 1970, *magna cum laude*, earning a B.A. degree in Biology and Chemistry. He then attended the University of Maryland School of Dentistry, receiving his Doctor of Dental Surgery degree in May, 1974. Upon completion of a general practice residency program in dentistry, he set up both a general dental and a hypnosis practice in Baltimore, where he practiced until 1989. Dr. Goldberg moved his hypnotherapy practice to Los Angeles in 1989 and retired from dentistry at that time.

In 1984, Dr. Goldberg received his M.S. degree in Counseling Psychology from Loyola College.

The American Society of Clinical Hypnosis trained Dr. Goldberg in the techniques and clinical applications of hypnosis in January, 1975. This organization trains only licensed dentists, physicians and psychologists in the use of hypnosis.

Dr. Goldberg has appeared on many television and radio shows throughout the country. He has conducted live past-life regressions on *Donahue, Oprah, Joan Rivers, Regis and Kathie Lee,* and on CNN and other stations.

Through lectures, television and radio appearances, and newspaper articles, including interviews in *Time* and *The Washington Post,* he has been able to educate many people as to the benefits of hypnosis. He has conducted more than 30,000 past-life regressions and future-life progressions since 1975, and none of his patients have ever been harmed through the use of these techniques. In addition, Dr. Goldberg distributes cassette tapes to teach people self-hypnosis and to guide them into past and future lives.

Dr. Goldberg gives lectures and seminars on hypnosis and regression and progression therapy as well; he is also a consultant to corporations, attorneys, and the local and network media.

For information on self-hypnosis tapes, speaking engagements, or private sessions, Dr. Goldberg can be contacted directly by writing to:

Bruce Goldberg, D.D.S., M.S.
4300 Natoma Avenue
Woodland Hills, CA 91365

Telephone: (818) 713-8190, or 1-800 KARMA 4 U (1-800-527-6248)

Please include a self-addressed, stamped envelope with your letter.

INDEX